Me and My Canoe

Me and My Canoe

BRAD BIRD

PEMMICAN
PUBLICATIONS
INC.

Cover photograph by Mark Bergen
We thank the Opasquia Times of The Pas, Man., for permission to use portions of stories that first appeared in the newspaper.

Pemmican Publications gratefully acknowledges the assistance accorded to its publishing program by the Manitoba Arts Council, the Province of Manitoba – Department of Culture, Heritage and Tourism, Canada Council for the Arts and Canadian Heritage – Book Publishing Industry Development Program.

Printed and Bound in Canada
First Printing: 2006

Library and Archives Canada Cataloguing in Publication

Bird, Brad, 1959-
        Me and my canoe / by Brad Bird ; with Mark Bergen.

ISBN 1-894717-35-X

        1. Bird, Brad, 1959- --Travel.   2. Bergen, Mark--Travel.   3. Canoes and canoeing--Canada.   4. Canoes and canoeing--United States.
5. Canada--Description and travel.   6. United States--Description and travel.   I. Bergen, Mark   II. Title.

GV776.115.B57 2006   917.04'54   C2006-906335-4

PEMMICAN
PUBLICATIONS
INC.

Pemmican Publications Inc.
Committed to the promotion of Metis culture and heritage

150 Henry Ave., Winnipeg, Manitoba, R3B 0J7, Canada
www.pemmican.mb.ca

DEDICATION

This book is dedicated to the spirit of the paddler.
May it endure forever, and help preserve our wild places.
It is also dedicated to my parents, Doris and Clayton Bird.

Brad Bird can be reached at birdbrad@hotmail.com

CONTENTS

PROLOGUE

"Brad, there's another canoeist here."

"OK, Lana, I'll be out in a minute."

It was the summer of 1991. As I sat in my editor's chair at the *Opasquia Times* in The Pas, Manitoba, it seemed that every canoeist in the world but me was fulfilling his or her dream of the Big Trip. I'd interviewed 65-year-old Edward M. Sears, a retired Ottawa civil servant who had paddled from Ottawa on his way west. He wrote interesting self-published accounts of his adventures. There was Alec Ross, a young man on a similar trip who wrote *Coke Stop in Emo*. A fellow journalist, he and I had a good visit. Others were doing smaller journeys, some by bike, others on foot.

What had got into people? Maybe the easing of the political situation had something to do with it. The Berlin Wall had fallen two years earlier, the Soviet Union was collapsing, and the threat of nuclear annihilation seemed remote for the first time in my 32-year lifetime. We breathed easier. People seemed eager to break free, like all those former Soviet republics, and live their dreams.

In 1981 Terry Fox had stared cancer in the face and run across much of Canada before his foe knocked him down. Imitators followed in Terry's heroic footsteps as they sought to raise funds to help find cures to cancer's dreaded diseases.

For me, the big inspiration was reading Don Starkell's *Paddle to the Amazon*. In June of 1980 Starkell and his two sons, Jeff and Dana, left Winnipeg on the Red River on their way to the mouth of the Amazon in South America. Some 20 million paddle strokes and 12,181 miles (19,603 kilometres) later, Don and Dana made it — the longest recorded journey by canoe in history. They had been arrested, shot at, robbed, jailed and set upon by pirates, as Don recounts in his book, edited by Charles Wilkins. "If we'd known we were going to make it, the challenge would not have been the same — we might not have gone," Don wrote. "If we'd known what lay ahead, we certainly would not have gone."

Adventure and the unknown were what I craved. I had no burning need to paddle to South America. New Orleans would do. After 12 years as a newspaper reporter/editor I relished the variety of stories that came my way each day. I'd won some awards. But as of late, I'd become stale. I wanted to be a story for a change. I wanted to do something worth writing about. Recording other people's adventures only whetted my appetite for one of my own.

The Pas was a great place to live, and I'd been there almost four years. I enjoyed working for publisher Murray Harvey. He was one of the smartest men I'd ever met. A perk of the job was use of the company van on weekends for canoe trips, so I didn't have to buy a car. Located on the Saskatchewan River, The Pas was in the heart of canoeing country. Henry Kelsey, Peter Pond, my ancestor James Curtis Bird and others of the Hudson's Bay Company had sailed past the townsite on their way west, centuries earlier. The pristine lakes of the Precambrian Shield lay a short drive north, past Cranberry Portage, and I'd made good use of Mistik Creek and other places for weekend adventures, as I loved to fish for walleye and northern pike. Trapping and commercial fishing country lay to the east, and I'd gone there with some friends from The Pas Reserve, Eric and Moses Bignell and Edwin Jebb.

I wanted — no, I needed — much more. Like those Soviet republics, I needed to break free and set my own course, a new course. In July I decided to quit my job at the end of August and paddle to New Orleans. There was an adventure! In New Orleans I'd buy an old car and drive home. The journey would begin at the town dock. The Saskatchewan would take me and my partner to some big water — Cedar Lake, Lake Winnipegosis, Lake Manitoba. The Assiniboine River led to the Red, which led to the Minnesota River, which emptied into the Mississippi. From there it was downhill to the Gulf of Mexico. (Later I would paddle from The Pas to Hudson Bay to span the continent.)

But who would be my partner? Usually it was Larry Grenkow of Winnipeg. He was an entomologist with Agriculture Canada and wasn't able to get away for the four months I figured we'd need for the trip. I turned my attention locally. At the Mennonite Church I'd seen Mark Bergen, the son of Pastor Ernie Bergen. He was young and fit. From the outset, Mark was as committed — some said as crazy — as I was.

In summary, the first leg of our journey in 1991 took us from The Pas to Le Sueur on the Minnesota River, and then from Dubuque, Iowa to Clinton, Ill., and from St. Louis to New Orleans, a paddle of some 3,700 kilometres. The second leg in 1995 saw me paddle mostly alone from The Pas north to York Factory on Hudson Bay, some 1,046 kilometres. The third and final leg came in 1997. Mark Bergen and I joined forces again for three weeks in July and paddled from Le Sueur to St. Louis, about 1,207 kilometres. Ice — which we were lucky to have survived — forced us to skirt this section in 1991.

All told, I've paddled some 6,000 kilometres across the continent, from York Factory on Hudson Bay to New Orleans on the Gulf of Mexico. (Mark has paddled from The Pas to New Orleans.) My days canoeing are among the happiest of my life. I think I was destined to live them. But how did I get to the point where I could undertake trips to New Orleans and Hudson Bay? What odd and wonderful things happened on the way? The rest of this account answers those questions. Hang on!

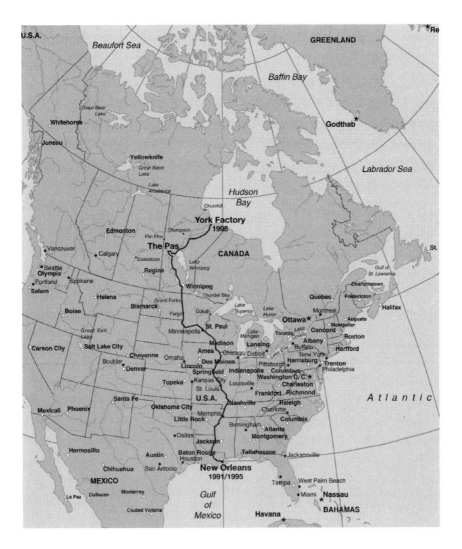

CHAPTER 1

OUR FIRST CANOE

"Has everyone drained their tank?"

My sister and I looked at each other. Kim and I knew who Mom meant by "everyone." We scampered off to the bathroom, excited about the trip to come. In the driveway of our home at 161 Grandravine Drive in suburban Toronto, Dad added last-minute items to our car, a little red Isuzu Bellet. Behind it sat a funny looking one-wheeled trailer covered with an old brown tarp that smelled of mildew and campfires, and in it were our big canvas tent, sleeping bags, air mattresses and other gear.

We were about to drive from Toronto to Boissevain, Manitoba, a week-long journey along the north shore of Lake Superior on the new Highway 17. Grandfather, Dr. F.V. Bird, lived in Boissevain, and we saw too little of him. I was nine and my sister six, and for us the five-week vacation promised to be a great adventure. Dad was a high school English teacher; Mom stayed home to raise us kids. For Dad, this was a rare summer when he didn't take courses.

It was 1968. Canada was a happy place then, having just celebrated its centennial. The Maple Leafs had won the Stanley Cup, Expo '67 was a great success, and unemployment was low. For most people, life was pretty good.

Little was I to know the trip would launch me on a life-long passion that would shape my future. To that point I had never seen a canoe (other than in books), let alone paddle one. Kim and I loved the water and would swim and play in it for hours. Dad had taught us to swim — using the hand-under-the-belly technique, dunk your face and learn to float — and I was pretty well drown-proof, she not far behind.

After a few days of travel we pulled into Sudbury — Nickel City — with its barren moonscape of Precambrian Shield, quite a change from the farm country and forests we had seen. As we followed the Trans-Canada Highway through town, Mom mentioned we needed some things. The Canadian Tire store up ahead would do just fine, so Dad wheeled our little outfit into the parking lot.

It was what I saw at the gas station *across* from Canadian Tire that caught my eye. A row of gleaming red canoes. Beautiful shapes. "Look at the canoes!" I blurted. "Oh, can we get one?" Mom looked at Dad as if to say, what do you think? I had a feeling this would be an especially good day. I didn't know it, but Dad was inclined to agree that a canoe might be a good thing for the family. He was an avid fisherman. He loved to go after pike and walleye. Rental boats aren't always available. There's only so much fishing you can do from shore. But with a canoe...

"We'll see," he said. Our shopping done, we crossed the road to check out the fibreglass craft. Solid and stable, but only 12½ feet long, light enough to carry. They were called Vanguard, and to my eye they were gorgeous. "Oh, please, please, please!" my sister and I chimed. "It would be so much fun to have one, and we could use it for fishing!" We didn't have to do much of a selling job, as they were quick to agree and pay the man. It cost about $130. Back to Canadian Tire for a roof rack, paddles and life-jackets, and the deal was done — the Bird family had a canoe!

Let me tell you I was one very pleased boy as we pulled out of Sudbury and headed into the watery wilderness of northern Ontario. It felt like Christmas. Kim and I even quit poking and teasing each other for a day or two, we were so happy about the canoe. That made it easier for Mom, who served as referee and judge when things got out of hand.

MAIDEN VOYAGE

What fun we had! After some dry-land instruction from Dad about balance and such, we launched the maiden voyage. The first time it hit the water was exciting. It floated so easily and lightly compared to the big aluminum boats we had rented in the past. I took the bow, as I would for many wonderful fishing trips. To me, riding in the canoe felt as natural as walking or running. But it was less work than walking or running — in fact, no work at all. I took my first awkward strokes with a paddle, but they weren't awkward for long. As we traveled towards Boissevain we camped in places like Killarney and Pancake Bay provincial parks, where that little boat gave us great joy.

Kim and I played with it at the beaches, paddling around and deliberately rocking it and falling out. The canoe was a big toy to us, as well as a tool for fishing. The more we played in it, the more at ease we felt.

Canoeing, I later learned, was in my blood. My mixed blood. In Toronto, my childhood friends included people of Chinese, Japanese, Italian, African and Middle Eastern descent. It was normal to see kids of different shades, and I was pure white by comparison. But not as white as I thought. Dark complexioned, I learned that I had Cree Indian as well as English in my background. I was a descendant of James Curtis Bird, my great-great-great-grandfather who was an important man in the fur trade. In 1816 he replaced Governor Robert Semple of Rupert's Land who was killed by Metis at the Battle of Seven Oaks near the Red River Settlement, which later became Winnipeg. (I often think that my high school history teacher should have taken that lesson one step further. But he never did say who took over from Semple.) Bird had come from England as a youth to clerk with the Hudson's Bay Company at York Factory in 1788. He soon took up with a Cree girl, whom he named Elizabeth after his mother, and they married in the country way — the native way, without a minister. They had many children. Bird was given a large grant of land in Manitoba when he retired — land known and enjoyed today as Birds Hill Park.

James Bird's sons worked for the Hudson's Bay Company as trip men. They paddled York boats up and down the Hayes River, and many other arteries such as the Saskatchewan River, to move furs and provisions such as kegs of liquor. Trip men were the grinders of the fur trade, the pluggers who made it possible for others to reap the financial rewards. Paddling 12 to 14 hours a day for the grand sum of 10 cents, these men (no women were involved) also carried heavy packs of furs and trade goods over the landing points, or portages, when rough water or no water meant you had to walk. Their life expectancy was relatively short, like that of an overworked honeybee, as the dangers of hauling the big York boats were considerable, and the work wore them down. As they paddled they often sang, hour after hour.

DOC BIRD

Dad's father, Frederick Valentine Bird, served Boissevain as a physician for 62 years. Boissevain is a little town in grain and cattle country south of Brandon, near the North Dakota border. Grandpa had been born on a farm beside the Red River north of Winnipeg in 1885, the year Louis Riel was hanged, and he died in 1977 at the age of 91. "Your grandfather was a half-breed," I was told by a Boissevain man, "and a darned fine doctor." He helped so many farmers that they put him in the Manitoba Agricultural Hall of Fame. My father, one of Doc Bird's two sons, was one-quarter native. The other son is my Uncle Mackenzie, who was quite a soldier in the Second World War with the Princess Patricia's Canadian Light Infantry. He fought through Italy and in northern Europe, with no injuries but 28 bullet holes in his uniform. It was a miracle he survived. He told me he didn't expect to. When his regiment came home, he led it. Grandpa married a nurse, Irene Bradley, the first white woman in the Bird line. She was gentle, slim and refined, and from her I got my name.

If my father and uncle were one-quarter native, then my brothers and I were one-eighth, as was Riel. Thus I was a Metis.

My father, without knowing it, lived the life of a Metis as a boy. Born Feb. 17 in 1919, he loved to roam the prairie sloughs and the big ravine north of Turtle Mountain, where he hunted and trapped after school. While most other boys stayed in town, Dad and sometimes his brother set out (in different directions) with their .22 rifles, often until after dark. Sometimes Dad made a fire to heat up a sandwich or cook a bit of duck or hare. Once, at age 14, he saw a fox some distance off, fired a quick off-hand shot with the fox on the run and drilled it through the ear. As there was no hole in the pelt, the fur buyer accused him of using poison, until he was shown where the bullet had ended up in the nose. Running jackrabbits often fell to Dad's rifle — once he bagged three in succession with one shot each — and later many deer.

War came. With his practised eye he figured he'd make a good fighter pilot, but the Air Force figured differently and made him a bomber pilot in 1943 at the ripe old age of 24. His first tour was as a flight instructor. His second was as an operational pilot. He and his crew flew 34 operations over Occupied France and Germany, including raids over the Ruhr Valley, a well-defended industrial zone. More than once, searchlights coned their four-engine Halifax III and he threw the plane into dives, which broke the hold of the lights and got them away from the flak, or bursting shells. One night, flak disabled two of their engines, but he still returned safely. In all his years of flying he never bent an airplane. These and other scrapes, as well as down time with his crew, forged strong bonds among them. My book *Nickel Trip* recounts this story.

HARMONY AT HOME

Dad was always in work, first as an Air Force pilot until retirement in 1964 and then as a teacher (he left the Air Force on a Friday and began his new career the following Monday). He and Mom made stability and love the hallmarks of our home. I never knew them to fight, though they must have squabbled. They kissed and hugged when Dad got home, wearing his Air Force blue, and their example set the tone for the rest of us. My three brothers were much older than I, so we rarely mixed, let alone fought. (I remember Bill taking me kite flying and swimming, and Bob treating me to the original *King Kong* movie, but that's about it.) My sister and I squabbled, but for the most part our home was tranquil. It was a surprise to learn about the tensions and rivalries that characterize some families. It was hard to learn to deal with conflict in relationships, as I had seen so little conflict between my parents, though I had the usual scraps with childhood friends.

Mom, Doris Aconley, had worked at Eaton's in Winnipeg before meeting father, Frederick Charles Clayton Bird, at a dance. Her father, William Aconley, was a carpenter and noted dog trainer who operated Ainville Kennels. Her brother, my Uncle Bert, eventually took over the business and diversified into horses, raising some national champion appaloosas, including Mouse and Buttons. Mom's mother, Zillah Taylor of Driffield, England, had come to Canada on her own as a young woman — a bold move in the early years of the 20th century. Her family was in industry. Unfortunately for me, both of Mom's parents died before I was born.

On Sept. 13, 1941, Doris Aconley and Clayton Bird were married in the big Anglican Church on Osborne Street in Winnipeg. Seven weeks later he went overseas to war, and he was gone for three years. Of course, both changed in the interim. They weren't sure they could make it work when he returned. But they did. The first three boys, Bill, Bob and Bruce, were born between 1947 and 1953. I arrived six years later, a little surprise when both my parents were 40. Kim was three years younger than I, and we adopted her when she was two (a special day for us all). Our parents, then, had two groups of children: the first three sons, and then Kim and myself.

Mom was never one to mix much with neighbours, but she did take in children for lunch and after school. She was always there for us. She told me the most rewarding years of her life were those spent raising her children. Our parents were like two wheels of a bicycle: family wellness depended on both. Sometimes I think Mom spent too much time in the house and not enough with other women and other activities. I think she would have been happier with a wider circle of friends and interests, and she did tend to get down.

One thing that perked us all up was summer camping. Mom was as excited as we were about the trip to Manitoba. With our new canoe, we traveled up and around Lake Superior, and spent a memorable number of days at Sibley Provincial Park near Thunder Bay. One evening at Sibley we sat around a fire with an American couple. The talk turned to fishing, and Dad mentioned that we were interested in northern pike — big ones, if possible. "I'll tell you what," said our new friend, "there's a honey of a little lake not far from here. But you have to carry everything into it. There's no road."

That suited us fine. We moved our tent trailer to the wilderness campsite close to this lake, which was called Milkshake. Next day Dad and I set out on an adventure. It involved a two-kilometre portage, or carry, along an old trail through the boreal forest of the Canadian Shield. Dad carried the canoe and a paddle or two, and I, a skinny little guy, followed along with the rest of our gear — tackle box, fishing rods, lunch bag. I looked, and felt like, a loaded-down donkey. I tried my best not to slip on the dark green mosses covering the billion-year-old granite. Of course I did slip occasionally, and learned early that a turned ankle is a painful nuisance in the wilderness. Through stands of spruce and birch, over sharp rocky outcrops, up and down hills we plodded, not knowing what to expect at the end.

What we found was a small bay at a creek mouth. The water was clear, but brownish black in its depths. Spruce trees had fallen into the lake, like spears jutting out to protect its rocky edges. "Let's hope this lake has a few pike in it, Brad," Dad said in his usual understated way. Soon we were on the water, and there were no other boats; good! I liked it that way. Thirsty from our sweaty carry we dipped our cups and lifted up some cold and sweet-tasting refreshment. "OK, get fishing," Dad announced, as he propelled us at a nice trolling speed just outside those fallen spruces. I slipped on a No. 3 Mepps silver spinner and not a minute had passed before we had a strike.

I'll never forget that first pike from Milkshake Lake. It struck hard, bending my rod almost double. It ran toward the underwater branches, but Dad pulled us into deeper water in time to avoid a tangled mess. Excited, I turned the handle and gained on it a bit, but the pike ran in powerful bursts, making the drag of my Mitchell 300 scream. Away from the trees, it bull-dogged deep like a walleye. I hung on, amazed by the power of this wilderness fish, determined not to lose it. Then to my surprise it swam beneath the canoe to the other side, rubbing my line against the fiberglass. "Keep your line off the boat," Dad warned, "or it will break." I did as told; our line was only eight-pound test. However, it seemed the fish had more control over matters than I did! After a minute or two of further struggle we saw the pike at the surface some distance out — chunky and dark, like an approaching alligator. "Keep him down, Brad, or he'll throw the hook." Indeed he shook his toothy maw once or twice before I pulled him lower into the water. Now the fish came in calmly; we'd won the fight. But this was a ruse. At sight of the boat it ran in another explosive bid for freedom, almost tearing the rod from my hands, the reel whining again. At Dad's urging I kept the rod tip up and at right angles to the line, to let the rod take the strain. I prayed the line wouldn't break and again attempted to ease the fish toward him. This time it worked, as Dad reached down and hoisted the muscular beauty behind the gills. "A nice four- or five-pounder, Brad," Dad said, smiling, while freeing the hook with forceps. "Good stuff." We both smiled as he put our fish on the stringer and trailed it behind the canoe.

FISHERMAN'S PARADISE

Soon I had another. And then another. They all went about two kilograms. Not wanting to miss the fun, Dad started fishing too, casting out with his little blue rod, which he had shortened for use in the stern. He paddled and we trolled. Sometimes we had two on at once. That made for some interesting moments! If there was a fisherman's paradise in those days, Milkshake Lake was it. We went back about three days in a row, releasing far more than we kept.

One time things went sour. As we rounded the far corner of the lake I hooked and then lost a nice fish as the line broke. "Don't worry about it," he said. "We'll go back and catch him again." Even my strong childhood faith in my father couldn't quite wrap itself around that one. Catch the same fish again? It seemed unlikely. I'd never seen or heard of it done, even on TV's Red Fisher show, which is what we had for fishing shows in those days. (And I much prefer it to the commercials that masquerade as fishing shows today.) But I did as told and put out the line. We turned around, trolled over the same spot, and soon I had a strike — fish on! It fought with typical vigour. "Easy now," Dad said, as I brought it close to the boat. Up it came in his grip — a nice five pounder, according to our scale — and dangling out the side of its mouth was my Mepps spinner with the broken line. We shared a good laugh, and my faith in father's words was pretty well impregnable after that.

On the way back I struggled on the portage with the added weight of at least nine kilograms of fish. I think Dad saw that as a lesson for me: take only what you can use, because you've got to pack them out and clean them too. I also learned the value of fish as living things deserving of respect. (It bothers me to see them shown anything less.) Back on the bigger lake where we camped, we paddled to an island near shore. "Bait up, Brad. This kind of structure is good for pike. They like to sit in these narrows and wait for food to come along." Just as we passed through that narrows, something big struck. My rod bent sharply, and I struggled with the fish as best I could. Dad could see my wrist was like jelly after fighting all those Milkshake monsters, and he took my rod and landed a 10-pounder. That made the day. Biggest fish I'd ever seen. We paddled home feeling like heroes. I did, anyway. Even my little sister was pretty impressed. Mom enjoyed eating fish and she too was pleased.

Not all our trips turned out like that one, though. One time we saw a creek heading into the forest. We decided to follow it, hoping to end up at another place like Milkshake. It wasn't to be — it was just a stream that petered out after a mile or two of struggle. Still, that little red canoe made our attempt possible.

After these fishing adventures, visiting Uncle Bert on his farm near Winnipeg and my grandparents in Boissevain was a bit of a letdown. Grandma was bedridden. It was sad to see her so weak. Grandpa looked after her, and us. He lived in a big white house at 710 Stephen St., where

Dad and Uncle Mack had grown up. Grandpa's kitchen had a smell all its own, part carbolic acid and part dinners from decades past. We ate roast venison. My sister and I consumed vast quantities of his raspberry and saskatoon preserves. "You like grandpa's saskatoons, eh?" he would chortle, as we stuffed our mouths and nodded. Then we'd all drive out to Turtle Mountain to pick some more.

Good memories. That's how I came by my love of paddling and camping, through my genes and through a childhood steeped in outdoor fun and education. Paddling became a passion once we got that little red canoe. It became a passion that later overrode other concerns, such as making a living. It was a passion that would launch me on a quest to paddle the length of North America, from York Factory to New Orleans, some 6,000 kilometres.

But first I had more learning to do.

CHAPTER 2

OUTLET BEACH

That little canoe survived our first fishing trips with just a few scrapes. I arrived home from that Boissevain journey feeling like a seasoned voyageur.

Usually we camped closer to home. Our favourite destination was Outlet Beach Provincial Park in Prince Edward County, south of Belleville. With its three kilometers of white sandy beaches on Lake Ontario, beautiful campsites, pony rides and miniature golf course, this park had a lot to offer. (The "dinosaur tracks" painted on the road leading in were a source of wonder when we were small.) A channel connected the beach and Lake Ontario to East Lake, where we did most of our fishing. Naturally, the channel helped to keep that fishery healthy.

Summer fishing trips began after daybreak, with me peering over my sister to see if Dad was awake. When I finally caught his eye, the next trick was to ease out of my sleeping bag and crawl over Kim without waking her, slip on my runners and unzip the door. Dad and I then made our escape in the car toward East Lake, a few minutes away. If Bruce or Bob were with us, they often came along.

First stop: Martin's Marina. There we rented a big steel boat, or used the plywood car-top boat Dad had made. Mr. Martin — I never knew his first name — was a tall slim chap in his late 50s with a deeply lined face who loved the outdoors. He was the type of man whose face graced the cover of *Outdoor Life* magazine, to which we subscribed. Mr. Martin usually had a pipe in his mouth and a pleasant but short greeting for a boy. He liked kids, and had rigged a diving board near his marina in the channel. At Martin's we bought the gas and oil that were mixed for fuel. For me, the smell of gas was synonymous with fishing. At home in Toronto I'd catch a whiff of it in the garage and think immediately of good times.

Fueled up, we'd head out into the channel that opened onto the lake. Soon we started trolling, or dragging lures through the water at a low speed. Largemouth bass, smallmouth bass, crappies, sunfish, walleye, pike, catfish — East Lake had them all in abundance. Often we'd catch each species in a morning. I remember Bruce pulling in sunfish on a lure called Pikey Minnow that was twice as long as they were. I remember him and Bob having fish on at the same time, and trying to keep their lines from tangling. After we worked that shoreline up and down a few times, Dad opened up the motor and took us farther down the lake. On our left was Foster's fruit farm. I remember Dad lining up a barn on one shore with a bluff of trees on the other shore so we knew where to troll for walleye. Electronic fish finders? They didn't exist then, but we would have dismissed them as an unfair advantage and totally unnecessary.

When the fish weren't biting, Dad had a trick that always seemed to work: he'd open up the big green metal tackle box and announce that it was time for a chocolate bar. That was about the only time I ever ate a chocolate bar, believe it or not. Often I hoped the fish wouldn't bite so that I could bite into a Coffee Crisp or Oh Henry, so there was some suspense involved. Dad made no secret of buying them (usually at Martin's); they were part of our fishing arsenal and strategy. The only question was how long it would be before we got to eat them. Strange thing was, it seemed to work: the fish almost always began to bite during, or after, our snack.

It was a big day when I was first allowed to steer the boat. I would've been eight or nine, and it made me feel pretty grown up. At my command was the power of our 5.5 h.p. Evinrude, 1950s vintage. We also used a smaller Scott-Atwater motor. You had to steer around logs and other boats, so I took the job quite seriously. Usually the weather was fine, but if the morning turned windy or rainy I would relinquish my place at the motor and crouch under the bow. It was cozy there as I curled up on a life-jacket or coat, the boat pounding slowly through the swell. Over the years I likely spent hours there, peering back at Dad at the helm, as much at peace with myself as a boy could be.

We also camped at the Outlet each autumn. It was cool, but we bundled up in sweaters and slept in double sleeping bags. Sometimes my brothers came along, for they loved to surf those Lake Ontario breakers almost as much as I did. The waves rarely amounted to much in summer, but come fall they were big.

Each September we'd be almost alone in the park, as the cool weather and school term kept most people away. My parents thought nothing of packing up Friday after supper and heading out from our Toronto home on the 2½-hour drive to Outlet Beach. Most of our gear was ready to go, so it was just a matter of packing some food and such. It was usually dark when we arrived, and we sometimes had a fire, though often we kids got straight into the sleeping bags. I always looked forward to that. There was something special about the cool night air, the familiar comforting forest smells of those bags (with all the lingering odours of past camping experiences), the close proximity of my sister who could easily be kicked or teased (and who took equal liberties with me), the scent of sand and Lake Ontario and the soothing, rhythmical sound of the big waves breaking. Next day, we'd be riding them.

MOM EATS A SPIDER

Breakfast while camping was always Dad's job; mom deserved a rest from all her duties at home. Maybe that's partly why she enjoyed camping so much — though one time, around the campfire, she pulled what she thought was a lump of hot chocolate powder from her mouth and put it on the table. "It" was a large spider, which got up and crawled away, amid much laughter and a few squeals from Mom. Typically we'd have pancakes — big, fat Aunt Jemima pancakes dripping with maple syrup from Clifford Foster's nearby farm. There would be fried eggs too (steamed with water that made them tender), lots of bacon, and often fried tomatoes, sweet and zesty. After such a repast my brothers and I were ready. Cool though it may have been, the leaves stripped from the poplars by brisk September winds, we pulled on our swimsuits and took the canoe to the beach, bursting with anticipation.

You haven't lived until you've paddled a canoe into the breakers of Lake Ontario. They developed slowly, starting well out, swelling over the hard sandy bottom of the bay and crashing violently in the shallow waters along the beach. Those waves were incredibly noisy (I can still hear them in my mind), but even they couldn't drown out the screams of joy from my brothers and I as we surfed them in our red canoe.

We paddled hard from the start, for sometimes the waves broke over the bow and you had to turn the boat over to dump the water out before you really began. Being the smallest, I rode up front, while Bob and Bruce took turns in the stern. The first blast of cold water always hit me, of course, which raised a certain mirth with my brothers. "Keep paddling, Brad," they would shout, laughing, as I sputtered and shivered. It was good to know the big fire on shore was awaiting our return. Our camp was always only metres from the beach, behind the first bluff of poplars. Mom had the big beach towels handy, too. Sometimes I wonder how she ever let us do this stuff.

If we got past the first big breaking waves, we knew we were on our way. The next stage was to paddle on the swells about to break. The bow of the canoe, with me in it, would rise high, and then fall with a slam into the valley below. I only weighed about 40 kilograms soaking wet, but we broke the front plywood seat at least once, we landed with such force. That's when I usually screamed a mix of joy and alarm. We'd paddle out even farther until we figured we could turn around and get a good head of steam going. Then the fun really began. Paddling hard, we'd catch the crown of a swell and ride it like a surfboarder, shooting into shore like a bullet. Sometimes you capsized, sometimes you didn't. It was pure fun either way. Then we'd do it all over again, and again.

I didn't know it at the time, but this was an important part of my canoeing education. I learned what a canoe could do in rough water (it can do a lot). I learned what a powerful force water is (you shouldn't fight it) and I learned to have great respect for water. I learned that shallow bays create the biggest waves (something like people), and not to fear water but to accommodate it, understand it, work with it, to help your craft stay afloat and enjoy your time in its element. All of this knowledge would serve me well in the years and adventures to come.

CHAPTER 3

FOSTERS' FARM AND LARRY

In 1975, when I was 16, our family moved from Toronto to a little home near Cherry Valley, close to the Outlet Beach. We loved the area, had friends there, and had spent wonderful times camped there. Concerns about traffic and crime in Toronto convinced Dad it was time to move — we'd been there 15 years — and when he got a chance to teach at Prince Edward Collegiate in Picton, we bought a place on East Lake.

At East Lake, Kim and I were introduced to the rural lifestyle, a lonelier life than we'd known in the city, where friends and activities had always been close. In Toronto, my friends and I made go-carts from scrap lumber and baby carriage wheels and raced them down a sidewalk. We played war games with guns we made from broken hockey sticks. Mark Davis, Keith Wright, Tony and Johnny Petriglia and others played hockey on our driveway for countless hours, initially with my sister in net (that didn't last long). We argued over who got to be Dave Keon, Ronny Ellis or Bobby Orr. (In net, I was usually Bruce Gamble.) For a change we came inside and played Monopoly, or had fun with my slot-car set. On Saturdays we joined Mark's Dad to watch Whipper Billy Watson wrestle on TV, and snuck peaks at the girlie magazines in their basement. I delivered papers each day after school for the *Toronto Daily Star*. Once we were driven to Yorkdale Shopping Centre to see a movie. We walked to a store on Keele Street to buy Orange Crush and Coke in small glass bottles shaped like Marilyn Munroe, and we hung around a Dairy Queen to talk, nervously, with girls.

Suddenly that world was gone. At East Lake, neighbours were far away. Winters were for school, snowmobiling and ice fishing. Summers were filled with work at Clifford Foster's farm, which featured a maple sugar operation, dairy cattle, apple orchards, a market garden and fruit stand. In June the strawberry patch needed pickers. It also needed a young man to carry the cartons of berries to the old Allis Chalmers tractor that hauled them to the fruit stand. People would stop, chat with Clifford or his wife Margaret, or Harold, Clifford's father, and buy berries, corn, potatoes or maple syrup. For a boy it was a wonderful place to work. Clifford and Margaret were easygoing, cheerful and forgiving souls. And Margaret was a great cook. I was starting to fill out a little and appreciate food a lot more than I had.

They had two sons, Dean and Stewart, and a daughter, Roxanne. Dean was older and bigger, Stewart smaller but in some ways tougher. Both had strong characters. They scrapped a fair bit, both verbally and physically, and this was new to me. It was as if there was a contest between them in every activity. They kept each other mentally and physically tough, and as I watched them I learned something of the dynamics that characterize other families.

Together with Clifford and various other men and youth, we began hauling hay and straw late in the berry season. I always looked forward to the call, in early July, to help in the fields. It was a real man's job, tossing square bales all day (they were actually rectangular), and I knew the girls in the berry patch looked at me with greater respect when I was elevated from their world into the world of heavy hay and men. We boys learned to work like men by watching them, listening to them and imitating them. To their credit, most of the talk was clean and healthy, and I think Dad knew what he was doing when he spoke to Clifford about my possible employment.

❧

This, too, was a good education. I learned how to work hard, hour after hour, despite fatigue, and I developed some of that sinewy strength that is so important to long-distance paddling. A weak paddler is at risk of injury, and there was little room for injury on a trip down the Mississippi River, which I had in my future.

Haying involved risks, of course. One time in the mow of the barn I was taking bales thrown to me by a neighbour man off the elevator. Whether by design or accident he caught me square in the face with one, and that smarted. And you certainly didn't wear shorts while haying, as some of the bales from low spots were heavy with moisture, requiring use of the thigh to get them on the wagon. And then there were telephone and hydro lines to contend with. We piled those wagons high with hay and straw, and many a time I had to duck under lines or tree branches as we rode back to the old wooden barn.

THIRSTY AS HORSES

It was a lot of fun. After loading and unloading a wagon we'd head to the house where Margaret had watermelons ready for us to devour. We'd be dripping wet with sweat, and hungry and thirsty as horses, and in that state few things have tasted as good to me as those large sweet pieces of watermelon. We slurped and we burped and we slurped some more. Afterwards, pumped up by the work and our thirst slaked, Dean would pick up the makeshift barbell (the axle and wheels from an old tractor) and we'd see who could do the most presses. Stewart was often a winner, for he was strong and determined to outdo his brother. He went on to become a champion wrist wrestler out west.

Clifford was a bit of a character. He always seemed to have a smile on his face, or a funny story to tell. He always had time for people. And he was a practical joker. One time, we were checking the electric fence that kept some cattle corralled. It was just a wire held in place by some posts, but Clifford and I stood in a low spot — a wet, low spot. We stood in water. "Just grab that thing, Brad, and see if it's working." We used to do that and get a little jolt. But, standing in water, the jolt was pretty stiff, and as I jumped a bit, he broke down laughing.

Could he ever work. Clifford was stocky and strong, and he set the bar pretty high when it came to throwing hay, for example. Clifford was always on the wagon, stacking the bales we gave him. Harold, his father, a slender and soft-spoken man with massive hands, usually drove tractor. A lot of Clifford's work was up and over his head some distance. It took three of us to keep him supplied with bales. We all sweated buckets and it felt pretty good. I'll never forget the time a young man from Quebec came to work at the farm. It wasn't easy for him as he was from the city. I learned some choice French words that summer in the old hayfield!

Then there was market day, Saturday. It began before sun-up when we picked about 20 bushels of corn. The ripe ears snapped off with a crack, and the plants were taller than we were. I enjoyed filling and hauling those heavy baskets partly because I knew I was getting stronger, and partly because it was fun to work as part of a team. While the boys and I picked corn, Clifford milked the cows, which he referred to as his "girls." The day before market, we picked tomatoes and dug potatoes. Depending on the season, we also sold strawberries or apples, which also had to be picked. Transparents were a sweet early yellow apple that I savoured. Working from an old wooden ladder, I filled many baskets of these, while in the tall grass below Tiger the Great Dane slept. When the big red farm truck was finally loaded, we drove the 40 minutes north to Belleville, where we parked downtown in a lot reserved for farmers. Like many others, we soon had makeshift tables set up and produce displayed. Familiar faces bought corn, a baker's dozen (13) for $1. A four-quart basket of tomatoes cost about $1.50, much the same as potatoes. We were busy, Margaret, Clifford and I, packing produce in bags and making change and chatting. Often people told us how good the food tasted; no wonder, it was fresh! What a fun and busy time we had. For all this, my first summer, at age 14, I was paid $20.

At East Lake, Dad and I got into beekeeping, thanks to a man named Willie Fraser. Willie sold Dad six hives, which we kept at Fosters' farm. The farm benefited from the pollination as the bees went from apple blossom to apple blossom collecting pollen, and we ended up with bumper crops of honey. Bees could be testy, though. I'll never forget the day we were extracting (removing the honey from the frames), when the bees took particular exception. I was stung a number of times and ran through the maple bush in one direction, while Dad high-tailed it in another! Mostly, though, with Willie's coaching, we and the bees got along fine.

High school came and went. To celebrate our graduation, a boyhood friend from Toronto and I paddled for a week in Algonquin Park. Luis Kaj and I ran out of food near the end and ate spaghetti mixed with peanut butter! It tasted great. It's not a good idea to rely on fish. They tend not to co-operate when you need them most.

I then did a BA at Brandon University, escaping to Lake Metigoshe near the American border for some fishing and paddling when I could. After an MA in Journalism at the University of Western Ontario in London (where I was born), I returned west in 1984 to accept a reporting position with the *Winnipeg Free Press*. Now I was making my own living and was fortunate to be close to superb canoeing country. The Whiteshell and Nopoming Parks were both only a few hours' drive away, and that's how I came to meet Larry and Noreen Grenkow.

Larry soon became my best friend and a constant companion on many Manitoba canoe trips. It was a wet and windy day when I first met the Grenkows. We were in Nopoming. Larry and Noreen were having lunch in their canoe — the one I now own and call Jimmy-Jock. I paddled over in the old Vanguard and soon we were chatting. It turned out we were both heading the same way on an overnight trip, so we decided to stay together for company and to help with portages, which we knew to be muddy. It was one of the best things I've ever done, for Larry has been a wonderful friend and paddling companion since that day in 1985. Though he hasn't been able to accompany me on my longer journeys due to job commitments, he played a key role in helping me learn to be a better naturalist and canoeist. Larry is an entomologist with Agriculture Canada and has a keen knowledge of plants and insects. He is also a first-rate photographer. His conservative and inquiring temperament also complemented my more aggressive approach to canoe trips. Our friendship was, and is, a gift.

MUD TURTLE LAKE

One of our favourite weekend getaways was to Mud Turtle Lake on the west side of the Whiteshell. In two hours we were there. We paddled a bit, made the portage and there was Mud Turtle, welcoming and windswept. That little lake served up some good canoeing adventures, for it was a fair size and held vast numbers of small pike. One time the hooks we cast landed within a few metres of each other and we caught the same fish, which took one hook and then went on to smack the other. We both hauled him in! That's a feat I've never repeated with anyone or heard of being done by any other pair of fishermen. We even camped there in the snow one winter weekend. This is notable because later, starting in January 2005, I would walk and run 1,600 kilometres from my home near Boissevain to Churchill on Hudson Bay to raise money for the Heart and Stroke Foundation of Manitoba, often sleeping in the snow.

Larry and I paddled around the Crowduck Lake canoe route, the Caddy Lake route, through Nopoming Park and Wallace Lake, up the Bird River into Ontario — we did it all when it came to that vast country east of Winnipeg. In 1986 I left my *Free Press* job to work overseas as a freelance foreign correspondent and that brought an end to our many weekend and week-long canoe trips. After that Larry and Noreen moved to Saskatoon, where he remains with Agriculture Canada. But we make a point of paddling together once a year whenever possible.

On July 18, 1999, we launched the Jimmy-Jock from the bridge on provincial trunk road 348 south of Carroll, north of Minto, for a three-day trip on the Souris River. It would end at Wawanesa 48 kilometres away.

The Souris River begins in Saskatchewan, snakes south into North Dakota and returns to Canada in southwest Manitoba, meandering through agricultural country and towns such as Melita and Wawanesa until it empties into the Assiniboine River and finally merges its waters with the Red River. Ultimately, that water enters Lake Winnipeg and pours into Hudson Bay.

PADDLING THE SOURIS

The Souris is small but sometimes spectacular. Not as wide as the Red or as wild as the Hayes, it nevertheless offers breathtaking beauty with sheer cliffs, sparkling rapids that invigorate even seasoned paddlers, towering cottonwoods and giant snapping turtles that reign supreme among the river's reptiles.

When Larry Grenkow and I looked for a three-day canoe trip that was close to my home, we didn't look beyond the often-ignored Souris. Used as a transportation link by the early fur traders, the Souris today is seen mainly by people from bridges. Seldom is its natural appeal appreciated as it should be: from a canoe, on its level, in its domain.

Only minutes after getting on the water at 9:40 p.m. that Sunday night, we were glad we had chosen the Souris. Two great horned owls barked at us in strange owly language neither of us had heard before. Then they flew from north to south across the river, only minutes after we had safely floated over the first of many sets of class-1 rapids we would see.

Swelled by recent rains, and by a spring that made the record book for local flooding, the river was in fine fettle as we briskly glided eastward. Its speed approximated that of the Mississippi, about five kilometers an hour. Needless to say, we didn't paddle hard this trip. And this night, with dusk setting in quickly, we chose a camp on the north side and made ourselves at home.

While Larry cooked supper, I set up the tent in a grassy area. It felt great to be back on the water, away from telephones and buildings, close to the earth and the animals. We agreed that this was the life.

During the night, a strange grunting sound, like a strong expulsion of breath, woke us. "What in the world is that?" we wondered. White-tailed deer will make that sound when confronted by something strange or threatening — in this case, our tent.

Next day we were on the water by 9:30 and enjoying once again the aggressive current. The river meanders a lot and we witnessed the erosion that had taken place that spring, when heavy rains caused the banks to slide away in places, toppling trees and revealing earth that lay hidden for centuries.

Rounding one bend, we came across such a cut bank. "Wait, Larry, let's go back, I think I saw something." We found a large bone in the mud near the water's edge. A few minutes later I saw something else. We returned and this time I pulled a bison skull from the mud. What an exciting moment that was! For some years I had yearned for such a find — a bison skull complete with horns, a relic of a romantic past, evidence of the thousands of bison that roamed this country only a moment ago in the annals of time.

With the skull safely stored, we ventured on, stopping at Larry's request to check out some wildflowers — and finding not only a purple meadow of wild bergamot, but also a thicket of saskatoons that gave us a wonderful feed of the purple berries. We took some with us.

Moving on, we came to an area with high cliffs. Scanning the river banks, we searched for more relics but turned up nothing. I was quite content with the skull we affectionately named Bill — Buffalo Bill.

Some two or three hours later we arrived at the bridge spanning Highway 10, between Boissevain and Brandon. Many times I had crossed that bridge thinking what fun it would be to paddle beneath it, and finally I was doing just that. We sped on, hardly paddling, just steering and navigating through the many small rapids on the way.

PURPLE CONEFLOWERS

We arrived at the Souris River Bend Conservation Area, a 2,000-hectare protected zone on both sides of the river that was home not only to animals, but also fields of wild flowers, most importantly Echinacea, or purple coneflower. Neither of us had seen so many. It was Larry who identified them. A hard day in the sun was forgotten as we walked among the beautiful flowers, whose roots are known to soothe the blues. In North Dakota, poachers were stripping the land of the plant as they sold them to companies for a quick profit. What an irony that the movement back to the land and natural remedies contained the seed of destruction for some plants.

That Monday night, our second, we camped near a stony flat that offered a nice grassy area for the tent. Again Larry cooked while I set up our sleeping quarters. We had another good sleep, with no animal intrusions this time.

Next day we headed off into what became perhaps the prettiest part of the trip, through the conservation area, which was free from cattle ranges and the damage those animals can do to the land — stripping them of green growth, knocking down trees, and denuding them of flowers. We were glad that cattle were barred from this area.

Suddenly it was as if we were somewhere else, maybe on the Colorado River. Steep cliffs continued to dominate the landscape. No buildings were seen. We heard or saw large snapping turtles slip into the river. We sighted deer. Two fawns at one point bounded off together on the left.

And it was hot! The sun seared our tender skin, which for the most part remained covered. Eager for a swim, we chose a shallow rocky run that provided good footing. We floated some distance, and then walked back and did it again, and again. Cool and refreshing and fun.

On our final night we left the conservation area and proceeded north of Highway 2, where we camped on the west side of the river, which faced a horse pasture — and three curious quadrupeds. One horse in particular, a gray one, stood watch as we set up camp. Larry stayed up to see the stars, but I had to hit the sack at 10:45 as the mosquitoes were pesky and I was tired.

We arrived the next day in Wawanesa at noon, and soon had a meal and swim at the Lions Park, a lovely campground and pool facility that made us feel welcome. My friend Dave Wall picked us up as planned and we headed home to Lake Metigoshe, refreshed and pleased with our Souris River trip. It wasn't the North, but it gave us a good adventure.

CHAPTER 4

THE PAS

In May of 1987 I returned from a four-month working tour across North Africa, during which I reported from the war in the Western Sahara and such other places as Libya, Malta, Algeria and Tunisia (where the Palestine Liberation Organization was then based). One of my first stops was the *Winnipeg Free Press* at 300 Carlton Street for a meeting with editorial page chief John Dafoe, who had published my work. To me he was always "Mr. Dafoe." As a young reporter I admired this journalistic veteran who wrote the lead editorials, who deigned to chat with a young entertainment writer on occasion, and who even let me pen an editorial or two. A curmudgeonly man, he shuffled with the stoop of one long bent over a typewriter or keyboard. One day in his office I shared my dream of reporting from abroad about politics and war, and he replied that he would have liked to have done more of that himself.

John Dafoe was a grandson of the legendary J. W. Dafoe. With his lucid prose, his refusal of honours and his defence and advocacy of freedom in all its forms, J. W. Dafoe became the most respected and influential Canadian journalist of his era (he lived from 1866 to 1944). His grandson had covered Ottawa and made his own name as a voice of integrity and conviction in support of free trade and a united Canada. Meeting with Mr. Dafoe over lunch, I had no intention or desire to return to work in Canada. This man I held in high regard expressed guarded approval of my early efforts as a foreign correspondent and then asked, "Where are you going next?"

My answer was northern Spain. I had met a Basque photographer named Zabi Otero while covering the conflict in the Western Sahara, where I felt very much at home despite the lack of water and canoes. Zabi invited me to visit him at his home in Spain. There I would write about the separatist movement led by a militant group called ETA (Basque for "Basque Homeland and Freedom"), and then return to Tunis to study French and Arabic. I carried out the first part of my plan, but when it came time in Madrid to buy a ticket to Tunis I lost my nerve. Things that day lost their focus for me; I'm not sure why. I ended up flying to New York and then to Winnipeg, much disappointed in myself and very sad. It was a low point in my life.

Months later, still numb and depressed, I applied for a reporting job in The Pas with the *Opasquia Times*. Though I landed the position I had doubts. Where in the world was The Pas? (Some 500 kilometres northwest of Winnipeg.) Why would I want to live there and work for less than half the *Free Press* salary? Should I wait for an opening in Winnipeg? But it was work in my field; I took the job. This, as I recall, was late in 1987.

MURRAY AND LORRAINE HARVEY

Murray Harvey owned the *Opasquia Times*, which came out Wednesdays and Fridays. A successful businessman, Mr. Harvey had taken over the paper from a previous owner who had failed to earn the support of the community. "You have to ensure that everyone who walks out that door is happy, even if they come in mad," he told me. It was one of many good lessons. Mr. Harvey was also a management consultant who worked with Aboriginal people. In my view his wife, Lorraine, was a key to his and the paper's success. She was a shrewd judge of character and very astute. One time, while I was in her office, we heard my two reporters begin to laugh. They were in the newsroom a short distance away, and I wasn't sure how my boss's wife would respond to laughter, when we were supposed to be working. I thought of the times I too had broken into laughter with them. "That's the sound you want to hear," she said, putting me at ease.

ം

Hired as a reporter, I soon had the editor's job when the other fellow left. I felt good, as the position carried some status in the community, and what a great community it was. Located north of the 53rd parallel on the edge of Canadian Shield country, The Pas was still rough around the edges, a frontier town known for mining and trapping and fishing. It was also known as the place where Helen Betty Osborne had been abducted and murdered. An Aboriginal student with a promising future, Osborne had been pulled off the street one night in 1971 and taken to Clear Lake north of town where she was stabbed with a screwdriver by some white teenagers. As evil as their crime was, it unfairly tarnished an entire population. When I got there you could still sense the stigma.

My relations with people got me over it. The town, I discovered, was full of good and hard-working people. Its mayor was Bruce Unfried, a cheerful civil servant. He ran the most efficient council meetings of any mayor I ever covered, saving me many hours of work over the years. I liked Bruce Unfried also because he took his son fishing. And he had courage. One time a delegation of influential homeowners showed up to criticize council for not paving their street. Mayor Unfried met them head on, saying it wasn't their year for paving, and if they didn't like it they could vote accordingly in the next election. Another man I valued was town administrator Tony Moule, who helped me with facts and background. His daughter Lisa, who worked for me, was a good reporter who went on to edit the *Opasquia Times*. Murray Harvey's partner was Dennis Popaden, who looked after the print shop. Dennis was always cheerful (despite occasional migraine headaches) and often had a story to share; he wrote a weekly column, as Murray did. One time while camping near Clearwater Lake Dennis had a visitor – a black bear – and his photos attest to how close he got. Possibly the bear was more concerned about Dennis than Dennis was of the bear! Just a fine man, and his wife, Jeanne, was his equal. It's odd how we sometimes don't realize how wonderful people are until separated from them by time and space.

Others I admired were involved in The Pas Elks Lodge. I joined at the suggestion of Mr. Harvey and found a group of committed people — among them Brian Bristow, Cliff Nichols and Harold Berg--who enjoyed the quiet work of helping children and adults in the area. We raised money through bingos and other means and then met to decide how to share the funds. I also covered the local farming community and came to respect people there as I had the Fosters. Then there was Ed Johanson. He was a spark plug of a man who fought for the Port of Churchill, which was under-funded. Eddie was capable of breaking out into song at any moment, and he had more spunk than 10 men. Herb Jaques and Sue Lambert were pillars of the annual Trappers' Festival. The Pas Friendship Centre was a busy and helpful place for Metis people, thanks to folks such as Sandra DeLaronde, a strong advocate for Metis people and women in particular. Eric Bignell and his brother took me trapping, which later became a way of life for me. These are among the citizens of The Pas who made me realize that the murder had been carried out by a small group who in no way represented the majority.

What also sold me on The Pas was its location in the heart of canoeing country, on the banks of the Saskatchewan River, which had been a major artery during the fur trade. Mr. Harvey learned of my love of canoeing and gave me a perk that smoothed the way for me to get on the water. On the alternate weekends I wasn't working I could use the company van and its gas to drive to any jumping-off spot I could find: Mistik Creek, Grass River, Clearwater Lake and many more.

By this time I had bought Larry's canoe, a bigger fibreglass craft than the old Vanguard, which I had outgrown. This "new" 16-foot (4.8-metre) canoe was handmade by Bill Brigden of Winnipeg, a former Olympic canoeist and master craftsman who produced many fine vessels. Brigden told me he had taken part in a 1967 trans-Canada relay paddle. He knew what constituted a good canoe: strength, light weight, fine lines and water worthiness. That canoe will handle any kind of wind or water if its paddler has any kind of ability. It is 29 years old as I write, and its retirement is not in my plans.

Oddly, my first impressions hadn't been good. It looked like a bathtub compared to my sleek little Vanguard. But my regard for that canoe grew in leaps and bounds as Larry and I completed one successful trip after another, in all kinds of wind and weather, without once feeling the boat let us down. Like a good but plain-looking friend, the Brigden canoe had hidden virtues. First was its strength. It could strike rocks in fast water and bear up to rough landings. Second was its flat bottom. Without a keel, this craft could be pulled laterally quickly, and turned on a dime. Third was its weight. "It's only 42 pounds," Larry told me. My old Vanguard, with its limited carrying capacity, weighed far more. The Brigden craft is heavier now as I write, due to patches and new layers of fibreglass resin, but remains easy to carry. Fourth was its ease of repair. Fibreglass in my opinion is an ideal material for long-distance wilderness paddling for the simple reason you can repair it quickly and easily anywhere. You can't do that with aluminum and I'm not convinced you can with Kevlar. Frankly, I won't undertake a long-distance trip in a boat I can't fix. To do so is foolish, for you're inviting trouble. Things do go wrong, canoes do break. You must be able to fix your craft or you're stuck. It's that simple.

PADDLING THE SASKERAM

One weekend I paddled the Saskeram Marsh area west of town at the suggestion of a man named Walter Koshel. Stocky, strong and a good woodsman, Walter was a true man of the North. He often competed for and won the annual King Trapper contest during the town's winter festival. Once he and a friend, Albert Ballantyne, snowshoed to Winnipeg. Walter was a family man like Bruce Unfried. I accepted his offer to guide us through the Saskeram on a 45-kilometre trip.

The paddle took us along Elm Creek, which runs into Sapaskoo Creek, into Sapaskoo Lake, along into Saskeram Lake and then to the Birch River, which took us to our finishing point at Bracken Dam. After a big lunch of turkey and trimmings made by Walter's wife Joy, we checked our gear and then headed for the Saskatchewan border in Walter's pickup on a Friday afternoon. Elm Creek was full of water, thanks to beavers. "Beavers sure help man out a lot," Koshel said, as we glanced at the dam a few feet away. "Of course they can be a nuisance, too, but more often than not they help a guy." We ate young thistle heads (the young flowers before they bloom) and they were good.

On Sapaskoo Creek, as we rounded a bend in the narrow waterway, we saw a cow moose. As we got to within 60 metres of her she turned and climbed the bank. "That made the trip right there," said Koshel, breaking minutes of silence. Then, seemingly in response, the moose let out a couple of grunts. Koshel replied in turn. Like many local men, he was a renowned caller of moose and geese. "Geez, Walter, I hope we don't call her back into the creek; this is where she got out," I said, thinking how little room there was to manoeuvre.

We paddled on, for we had miles to go before Pear Island, where we would camp. It became a running joke. "Where's that darned lake, Walter?"

"Shut up and paddle."

We were hungry and it started to rain.

"Where's that lake, Walter?"

"Shut up and paddle."

৯৹৶৻

Finally we found it as we rounded a corner. Then we took a "short cut" to Pear Island. This involved running into a thick wall of cattails, Walter climbing out and pulling the canoe in heavy mud, and us backtracking and cursing as the sun sank into the west.

"Where's that island, Walter?"

Finally we arrived. As I put up the tent, Walter got a fire going even though the wood was green and wet. (His tinder? Toilet paper). We ate soup, pumpernickel bread, and then the main course — a pan full of onions, drowning in butter and topped with a pound of bloody red beef in hunks and strips. The Queen herself didn't enjoy her meal more than we did ours that night, I guarantee you. We got home next day.

In September of 1990 I was invited by a local businessman, Terry Hendrickson, to accompany him and friends on a moose hunt on the Saskatchewan River west of town. With us were his father-in-law Mike Perchaluk and friend Lionel Levesque of Winnipeg. This offered a chance to explore some of the country along the Saskatchewan River. We went up river with Terry's big cruiser, with my canoe as cargo. His "Hood" was powered by a 270 h.p. V-8 — more power than many cars, and a stark contrast to what I was used to with the canoe.

At one point that first night, Lionel got up and let out a moose call that sent shivers down my spine. Five-thirty came quickly and the boys were dressed and gone. Before daybreak I too was down at the canoe with my shotgun. The Saskatchewan River shimmered in the early morning light and mist. A strong current challenged my paddle upstream to Barrier, where I found two men at a fire finishing breakfast.

Zachius Greenleaf and Tommy Ballantyne were commercial fishermen. Like me, they were headed to Barrier Creek to hunt. We talked about the abandoned settlement of Barrier, where Zachius had been born in 1941 but left as a teenager. He said the people moved away because there wasn't much to sustain them. The river barge, which had docked twice a week to bring supplies, was discontinued. The people grew old. The young ones wanted town life. And so the settlement became a relic to the fishing, trapping and hunting way of life, just as Warren's Landing, a Metis community on the north shore of Lake Winnipeg, became a relic to that increasingly rare way of life.

After paddling the creek and cooking a grouse at Barrier, I returned to camp and helped the men haul aboard a moose that Terry had taken. On the way home, Lionel told me he'd done a lot of good hunting in his day. I mentioned that he seemed to be in pain. "I've got cancer," he told me. "Liver cancer. I found out about five months ago. They figure a guy doesn't live much more than a year with it. It's too big to cut out." This gave me something new to think about — the importance of living each day to its fullest and not taking the future for granted. I would not put off my dreams.

And I was ready to live a new dream. This became clear when long-distance paddlers stepped into the office to tell of their trips on the Saskatchewan and across Canada. I enjoyed these interviews, but they left me itching for a journey of my own. One of these paddlers was Murray Edwards (or Edward M. Sears, his writer's name), a 65-year-old retired engineer and civil servant whom you had to admire for his pluck. Edwards had begun at Ottawa, had come across Lake Superior, and intended to continue much farther west. I have the first volume of his series, *North 49 West*.

Another paddler and fellow journalist was Alec Ross, who produced a book called *Coke Stop in Emo*. Alec was good enough to tip me off about the sad state of the Cumberland House fishery, which launched me on some of the more important work I did at the *Opasquia Times* about the harmful effects of hydro-electric dams. We enjoyed a pleasant evening of conversation at my place and I gave him a Mepps lure. He returned to the river with a bit of a heavy heart, as he wasn't looking forward to resuming his struggle against the strong current of the Saskatchewan.

Soon, I knew, I would take up a journey of my own. But where would I go?

CHAPTER 5

'CRAZY WHITE MEN!'

Paddle to the Amazon by Don Starkell answered the question of where to go. This is the incredible story of a man and his sons who paddled from Winnipeg to the mouth of the Amazon River. They went against the current of the Red, down the Mississippi, and across the Gulf of Mexico to South America. Now there was a canoe trip. I decided I'd be happy with a more modest objective: paddling the north-south distance across North America, from York Factory on the shore of Hudson Bay, near Churchill, Manitoba, to New Orleans. This the Starkells had not done. I set out to make it happen.

Early in 1991 I was into my fourth year as editor of the *Opasquia Times*. The publisher's son, Bob Harvey, had recently come aboard and was clearly being groomed to take over the paper. I had done about all I could there, and it seemed like the right time to move on. I was filled with such an excitement about the trip to New Orleans that there wasn't any choice — I *had* to do it.

The canoe, the gear, the skills — all were in place. What I needed was a partner. It could be done alone, but the trip would be more fun, easier and safer with a good partner. But who was free? Larry Grenkow was working.

Mark Bergen came to mind. I had been attending the Mennonite Church, where Mark's father Ernie was pastor, and had seen Mark from time to time at church, or when Ernie and Irene invited me home for lunch or supper. He was 19 and fit — but was he working, or committed to school in the fall? After church one day in July I approached him and told him about my plan. "Are you interested in going with me?"

His eyes lit up. "To New Orleans? You mean down the Mississippi River?

"That's right."

"Like Tom Sawyer and Huck Finn?"

"That's right, Mark," and I laughed a little.

"When would we leave?"

"September 1. That would allow us to get south before the snow flies, if we're lucky. I expect we'd be home by Christmas or a little later."

"Well, I was thinking of taking some college courses this fall — auto mechanics — but I'd rather do this."

"Maybe you want to think about it. It's a big decision. College is important too."

"I won't need a few days. I want to go! I'll get back to you later today or tomorrow, OK?"

Mark confirmed later that day that he was committed to the trip. His heart wasn't in auto mechanics; it was just something to do. His youth (I was 32) and athleticism were real assets, as the trip would be tough. He'd read Mark Twain and was as inspired as I was to paddle the fabled Mississippi.

Within days we lined up equipment for him, and I consulted my friend Wilf Monkman about a sail. Wilf was an old hand at bush work, having hauled commercial fish with horses in decades past and helped build various abutments and airports around the north. He knew something about everything and he knew just about everybody. Wilf thought a sail was a good idea and had a friend fashion a housing that clamped to my centre thwart to hold a rig in place. The sail itself was made by Sydney Burton of a rubber-fibreglass material.

JIMMY-JOCK THE CANOE

Next a name was needed for the canoe, and it had to be painted on the bow. "Jimmy-Jock" came to mind. An ancestor of mine, Jimmy-Jock was a half-breed, the eldest son of James Curtis Bird. Born about 1794, Jimmy-Jock had been a great traveler, which appealed to me in terms of a name. And for reasons we can only surmise he harboured a passionate dislike of things European. Sent south in 1820 to open trade with the Blackfoot, he liked their society so much he never left them, in the process infuriating the Hudson's Bay Company and American Fur Company, which he often played against one another for the best prices. This earned him enemies in both camps and it's a wonder he wasn't murdered. With the Blackfoot Indians he became a war chief with numerous wives. In 1877, though aged, he translated a treaty for his people at a gathering on the Bow River at Blackfoot Crossing. Jerry Potts was supposed to interpret, but some say he got too drunk. Jimmy-Jock died of natural causes, blind and toothless, with an old wife beside him, in a teepee, at the age of 98 in 1892.

A local artist painted "Jimmy-Jock" on the canoe, and we were ready to go. I consulted another friend, Albert Ballantyne, who knew the Saskatchewan River well, and he figured we'd have no trouble downriver. He wondered, however, about the wisdom of leaving so late in the season for an objective so far south. His words were prescient. I held off that long to save money for the trip and to prepare properly.

Sept. 1, 1991 was cool, sunny and breezy, and a crowd of about 20 assembled as we loaded our gear at the boat launch in the centre of The Pas. Mark's sister Tammy had been married the day before, and so she and other family and friends were present. I was focused on packing and looking after Athena, my cat, who was going with us at least as far as Winnipeg. I loved that little cat and wanted her along. Mark wondered about the decision, but a vet, Dr. Fletcher, had assured me that she could adapt.

Vicki Hornick of the *Opasquia Times* took pictures and notes as we got ready to leave at 1:30 p.m. Vicki and a young man who worked at the radio station rented rooms in my mobile home, so I had income while making the trip south. The newspaper also agreed to pay for weekly installments that I wrote and mailed home. A bonus was that Vicki liked Athena and was a friend of mine, and would look after her if I sent her back.

We packed light. Two plastic Action Packers held food and cooking equipment, an old duffel bag Dad used in the Second World War held my clothes, while a plastic tub loaned by a friend held Mark's. A five-gallon tub with snap-on top held valuables such as my camera. Everything was either watertight or would float, or both. We prepared for the worst but hoped for the best.

Finally, we shoved the canoe farther into the water and Mark climbed into the bow. I followed in the stern, we put the paddles to work, and we were off! It felt great to be leaving on a 4,800-kilometre journey to New Orleans! As my paddle hit the water for the first time I felt so free, so happy to be starting out on what promised to be a great and memorable trip. We shouted for joy as we got into the middle of the river and away from the people and rode the current toward Cedar Lake.

Athena wasn't as thrilled as we were. She shot me some glowering looks, but soon settled down. Her favourite place was under the splash cover, which was a tarp we cut to fit over the gunnels and held tight with bungee cords. But we didn't have it on yet, and paid a price. Dan Moore and his wife met us in their boat close to Big Bend, a rough curve in the river, and he advised us to take the north shore. We sliced through waves and took on some water. If we took on water in that bit of chop, I thought, could we manage the big lakes?

As it happened, Albert Ballantyne and two friends came along in a boat with a moose they'd just shot. "Cut them a chunk of meat," he said, and we got enough for two days. "Crazy white men!" Albert hollered as we headed toward New Orleans in a stiff wind. That about summed up his opinion of our chances.

The wind subsided at about 6 p.m. and by 7 we had sighted Wooden Tent, a cabin. The first night, after five hours of paddling, we camped there, about 32 kilometres downriver. The place belonged to Bill Bannock (a beloved fictional character created by Murray Harvey in his newspaper stories), but Bill of course wasn't around. We slept soundly.

The next day, Labour Day Monday, we covered another 61 kilometres and ended up close to Cedar Lake. One thing we lacked was enough drinking water. Fortunately we met a man who gave us some. We sailed a lot that day, whizzing down the Saskatchewan at terrific speeds. The sail that Sydney Burton made for us did a splendid job, but we added a second: our large Canadian flag. They were dynamite when the wind was right. We saw a black bear along the north shore, and a coyote.

It began to rain about 5, and we donned our raincoats. The splash cover kept the cat and gear dry, as we paddled on, finally coming to an old log animal shelter, in which we set up the tent, on the floor of wood chips and sawdust. The cat liked it, anyway. Unfortunately so did the swallows. Our neighbours were noisy.

The few pounds of moose meat that Albert gave us were eaten in two days of stew, as we worked up quite the appetites. From our shore that evening we could see Cedar Lake in the distance, a huge body of water.

TROUBLE LURKED

On Day 3 we awoke to geese honking and wolves howling. To speed our departure, we almost never cooked breakfast. Instant oatmeal with cold water (quite palatable) and a couple of hard-boiled eggs (cooked with supper the previous evening) sufficed, and we set off into a clear and breezy morning. But trouble lurked with the southwest wind, and although we made good time, our day's advance was halted at noon by high winds. We still weren't on Cedar Lake, but bogged down in the bays and wetlands approaching it.

We camped behind some willows for protection, tramping down the tall marsh grass for the tent. The rest of the day we dozed and read. Mark was into Rudyard Kipling's *Captains Courageous*, while I read Homer's *Odyssey*. About 3 o'clock the sky darkened and the wind picked up even more, so we scurried out to secure the canoe and our gear. Meanwhile, Athena got out and disappeared. The storm struck with predictable fury, with high winds and pelting rain, and we took refuge in the tent. Where was the cat?

I'd had Athena for a couple of years, since she was six weeks old. I'd heard about kittens being given away on a radio show called *Trading Post*, and she was the last one left. No wonder. As a kitten, she lacked whiskers and was small and homely, a kind of dirty grey colour. The guy threw in some food and a bowl to entice me to take her. She loved being warm. I'd come home from work to find a lump on my bed, under the covers, which moved, mole like, as she came out to greet me. She developed into a bit of a psycho cat, one that would frantically climb the blinds, run around wildly and even attack people. One time I left Athena with friends for a few days and found out when I returned that the woman's husband had fallen ill and she'd had to call an ambulance. The cat attacked the ambulance attendants. Maybe she thought they were going to hurt the old man, I don't know. She was different, that's for sure.

Cats do come back, and 40 minutes later our wet and humbled feline returned, much to my delight. A helicopter flew by twice, and we couldn't help but think they were looking for us. They may not have seen the tent, nestled into the grass and willows, but they would have seen the red canoe.

A highlight of the day was observing six otters in the river. They bobbed like corks, talked to each other like kids, and played.

On Sept. 4 we were on the water by 8, paddling hard. We headed east-southeast and finally got on to Cedar Lake, the wind at our backs. The breeze created swells, and Jimmy-Jock rode them well. Mark said it felt like a roller-coaster. What a thrill. We sailed a while, too. We learned that day that our splash cover was very effective at keeping out the waves, some of which broke over it. With the cover we were fine; without it we would have had to do a lot more bailing.

Athena enjoyed riding beneath it on the duffel bag behind Mark. She poked her head out periodically to see how we were doing, and seemed a happy camper. By mid-afternoon we made it to Oleson Point on a long peninsula, where Mark caught a nice pike, which we had for supper in a chowder.

This big lake had been crossed by many a fur brigade in the 1800s as they headed west with trade goods and then back to York Factory or Montreal with furs. Most of them, of course, had bigger canoes.

By day's end we were exhausted but elated. We'd come 46 kilometres down the lake — around islands, along points, sailing, paddling, even surfing the rollers at times. What a great day! We had almost done our first 100 miles.

We had been feeling low the day before, wet and wind-bound and, frankly, not sure where to go. But it all became clear that morning when we saw the sunrise, which told us where east was, and that we had a west wind — ideal. Easterville was close.

The people of Easterville had formerly lived closer to the mouth of the Saskatchewan, where fishing and hunting were superb, but Manitoba Hydro forced them out when the Grand Rapids dam was built in 1962. Their old community was flooded for the sake of cheaper electricity, largely to power southern industry and homes. Easterville people suffered from the dislocation as commercial fishing and trapping, their two key industries, were harmed. A big forebay flooded a vast area and held water as potential energy.

After riding more rollers toward the community we picked up a few groceries in Easterville and then accepted a "pickup portage" — a ride to Lake Winnipegosis in a truck with a couple of good guys, Mallory Umpherville and Dale Lavallee. They were impressed by our adventure and wished us well. When we got to the other side, a place called Denbeigh Point, we paused for lunch. Then we had a pleasant surprise.

Mark's father, Ernie Bergen, came along with a pot of delicious chili and buns. Ernie was good about the whole thing and didn't try overly hard to discourage us from going on. He thought I was a little crazy to have

My father, Clayton Bird, on a fishing trip in Manitoba in the mid-80s

Working at the *Opasquia Times*: reporter Vicki Hornick stands at right, Kurt Mueller is in the middle, while editor Brad Bird goes over some copy and appears to be wishing he were on the water. That was a very good newsroom staff.

Murray Harvey made the *Opasquia Times* a successful newspaper in every way.

Brad Bird (L) and Mark Bergen enjoy a breather before sailing from The Pas, Man. On Sept. 1, 1991

Here's Larry Grenkow. He and I have enjoyed some great trips over the years, in Manitoba and Saskatchewan. He's a good friend and an excellent naturalist. We try to do one trip a year together.

DEAR FRIENDS

Walter and Ida Koski

Wilfred and Beverley Monkman

The Saskatchewan is a beautiful river. Mark paddles in the stern while Athena shifts her bed on the Action Packer box.

Mark enjoys warming his feet after many hours of chilled toes, as October turned colder.

Brad fishes for pike on Cedar Lake. The cloud formations were particularly special as we paddled the 100-mile length of Cedar Lake, once a key segment of the east-west fur trade route. Mark caught a pike here; Brad got skunked!

Brad Bird (L) and Mark Bergen enjoy a breather before sailing from The Pas, Man. On Sept. 1, 1991

quit my job, but that's the price you sometimes have to pay to live your life as you wish. Since I had already quit a good job with the *Free Press* to follow my heart, I knew that things could turn out all right. My change of mind overseas had led to four happy years in The Pas. I had faith in the future and really wasn't concerned about what would happen after the trip. Things would take care of themselves.

With bellies full of chili, we got on the water by 3 p.m. and did 29 kilometres. Frankly, it was a little insane. After plowing into a west wind for an hour or more, and crossing 13 kilometres of rough open water to an island near the west shore, we headed south. The wind became a northerly, pushing us along.

Swells crested around us and occasionally on us. It was a wild and crazy ride, exhilarating. We felt so alive, because every moment counted. When waves broke over the splash cover I scooped the water off, struggling to keep us straight and trying all the while not to drop my paddle (though we carried a spare). It was thrilling and sometimes frightening, and reminded me of my boyhood days in the surf at Outlet Beach. Mark said how neat it was to sit up high on a swell and see the valley below.

"LET'S GO FOR IT"

It was Mark who suggested we head for an island some 16 kilometres away, after we made our initial long crossing. "Let's go for it," said my young bowman. "The island is south and we need to go south." So we did, riding a roller-coaster of waves. Athena, meanwhile, slept under the splash cover, a lump on the duffel bag.

What an incredible sight it is to look around you and see a sea of cresting waves, massive rollers on which we floated like a fisherman's bobber. What a feeling it was to be in sync with these waves, riding them safely but aware of that fine line. Above us, terns cut figures in the sky and squawked their greetings. Pelicans flew in precise formations, like military aircraft, their orange beaks and white-and-black wings vivid against the azure sky. We never felt alone on this vast body of water. It was like riding on a living creature. We were a flea on the back of a bear.

By 8 p.m. we reached our island, a crossing that took two hours. Close up it looked almost tropical, with large leafy trees creating a jungle effect. We were in the transition zone between the boreal forest of spruces and pine and the deciduous south with its aspens and birch. A rocky reef jutted out threateningly, but we poked around and found a way in. After a meal of chili and beans we slept to the sounds of breakers on the reef, a sleep well earned.

Next day, Sept. 7, we reached Mile 129 (or kilometer 208). By mid-afternoon we were wind-bound on the west shore of Lake Winnipegosis. A strong east breeze kicked up two-metre swells. We struggled in them for two hours that morning and made about 10 kilometres.

"This makes Cedar Lake look like a bathtub," said Mark at one point, as yet another wave broke over the bow, soaking him. I worked to steer Jimmy-Jock into another swell. Whoosh! And a wave broke over the cover in front of me, but the water spilled off the sides, not into the canoe.

All around us the lake was like a sea as swells built, crested, broke and rolled relentlessly to shore. In a way they represented life: we develop slowly, peak at our best, decline after that and coast to the shore of the Great Beyond. Above us, a few wispy clouds sat in the sky.

Stymied by the wind, we were about 64 kilometres from the community of Duck Bay, our next stop with a phone. Exhausted, we waited. Mark slept. We quickly learned that the weather was our master, not something to fight. It made sense in a lot of ways. It was not only safer but also easier and more productive to wait out the wind. What might take us three hours of hard paddling against the wind could be accomplished in an hour of easier paddling when it was calmer. We made a fire, dried Mark out — he took the brunt of the spray, being in the bow — and ate a hearty lunch. Athena hunted bugs on the stony shore as waves crashed and broke.

We were only a week into the trip, but it seemed like we had been doing this a lot longer. All was going well. We hoped our good fortune would continue.

CHAPTER 6

DOG ATTACK!

We began to feel a growing impatience to get south, quickly. The nights were cold and snow would soon be falling. Each day mattered, and Albert Ballantyne's words haunted us: "You're leaving it too late." We were in a race against time.

By next morning, Sept. 8, the wind had gone down, but it rained. It was Sunday, and we listened to one of Pastor Bergen's sermons on my mini tape recorder. By 10:30 we were on the water in our rain gear.

We paddled like machines for nine hours, not even stopping for lunch or supper. I made peanut butter and honey sandwiches for lunch and handed them up to Mark with my paddle. We ate so much peanut butter on our two trips down the Mississippi than I became allergic to peanuts.

Some distance from Duck Bay we met some commercial fishermen who were putting out nets. "You're taking on some pretty big water," one said. Yes, and tell us something we don't know.

We worked like dogs that day, determined to reach Duck Bay. Finally at 7 p.m. we were elated to see lights in the distance. We had reached Duck Bay and completed an estimated 260 kilometres since leaving The Pas. We were averaging 32 kilometres a day, not bad considering the fairly constant wind and rain. At Duck Bay we met Garnet Chartrand, who showed us great hospitality. We had our first showers, washed some clothes, and camped in his yard.

Next day dawned drizzly, windy and overcast, killing our plans to cross open water to Red Deer Point. We used our two sails, the one Syd Burton had made and our Canadian flag, but the flag at one point broke away, putting us in peril as the canoe lurched broadside to the waves. I quickly lowered the other sail too and we fought to get control. We took on some water, and it was a close call, but 30 minutes later we landed at a cow pasture. After lunch we slept, still tired from our 50-kilometre marathon the day before.

"Hey Mark, I'll walk up to the farmhouse and see if we can watch Canada play the U.S.S.R. on TV tonight. We might even get a meal out of it."

"That'd be great," he said, just waking up.

It wasn't a farmhouse we'd seen, but a commercial fishing depot called Good Harbour. There, Tabby and Robert and another man sat watching TV. They were friendly, and soon Tabby had four small walleye in a bag for us. We'd also been invited to return after supper to watch the game.

Back at camp we ate all four fish and then headed out for the game. At the shack, a different man asked: "Do you wear orange life-jackets out there?" We said we did. "Good, it'll make it easier to find your bodies."

"We've a comic here," I replied.

JOKER BROWN, PRIVATE EYE

"That's why we call him Joker," said Robert, who packed fish at the depot. Harvey (Joker) Brown, from Winnipegosis, was a fisherman and, of all things, a detective or private eye. He invited us to his houseboat, where we went over maps of the lake. He showed us where he had a cabin, if we needed it. Harvey, about 50 years of age, needed help setting nets and offered us a few days' work. But we needed to keep pushing on and declined. It was tempting, though. The game was a treat and ended in a 1-1 tie, thanks to young Eric Lindros.

Two days later we had our first setback. It came not from wind or water, or from rock or reef, but from a man and his dog. Sept. 11 was another drizzly day with a relentless south wind. We paddled until noon, when we stopped for lunch on Salt Point.

As we prepared to eat, an elderly farmer and his dog arrived in a pickup. The man, who walked with a cane, was friendly and curious, and Mark petted his golden Labrador retriever. It seemed OK. Athena was leashed to the canoe some distance away.

Suddenly the dog caught sight or scent of her and bolted toward the canoe, clamping its jaws around her mid-section while Athena screamed.

I ran toward them and tried to pry open the dog's jaws, then punched its head repeatedly, with little effect.

"Beat the bastard with your paddle!" I shouted, and Mark did so. That wasn't easy for him, as he loved dogs. Finally the Labrador got the message and let go. Athena was a mess, wet and snarling and obviously hurt. I undid her collar and covered her with my towel and shirt as she lay whimpering in the bottom of the canoe.

Grabbing my shotgun, I chambered a shell and warned the man to go, telling him I'd kill the dog if it returned. They went, with no further words. He had no control over his pet, as his feeble attempts to call if off during the attack went unheeded. Fortunately the dog was old, its teeth apparently worn. We saw no punctures on Athena, but feared internal injuries. And we were in no position to get a vet. So we waited.

My right thumb and nail had been punctured in the melee, bitten by Athena in her frenzy to escape from the dog. I cleaned the thumb as best I could and covered it with Ozonol. We built a roaring warm fire and made the best of a bad situation, staying there for the night, not wanting to disturb the cat.

Next morning Athena walked a little. She coughed up some food and bile, but no blood. It seemed she had used up at least one of her nine lives. While she was a bit better, my thumb was worse. It had swollen to twice its normal size and was red and sore.

❧

We paddled on, and I dipped the thumb in water with every stroke, hour after hour. That's what sucked the poison out and put it on the mend. The lake water was clean, and we drank it. The thumb remained big and sore for days.

At Meadow Portage we needed to cross a section of land to get to our next body of water, Lake Manitoba. We beached the canoe and walked to a roadway where a truck stopped, and we explained our situation to Douglas Bertnick, a sheriff's officer. "I know just the man you need," he said. I went with him, while Mark stayed with the canoe. Mr. Bertnick took me to the home of Walter and Ida Koski. The couple listened as Doug explained our situation, and then Walter Koski surprised me by handing me the key to his new truck. "Help yourself. Bring your gear back here and you can launch into Lake Manitoba from our yard. But first you'll join us for lunch and tell us about your trip."

WALTER AND IDA KOSKI

I was stunned by his trust. A new truck. He didn't know me. Bertnick was heading on, not going with me. We sure appreciate what Walter and Ida Koski did for us that day.

Mark was surprised, as you can imagine, as I drove up in the truck. "Let's load up!" I said. "Lunch is waiting." He couldn't believe it. We needed that jolt of good news.

Back at their home, Ida said to her husband, "The boys are making a trip you'd have loved, Walter."

"Yes," he said, "in my younger days." Our meal of chicken, pickles and bread was a nice change from our regular fare. We greatly enjoyed our time with this warm and trusting couple, and Ida, bless her, even tended to my thumb. But we had to keep going, the pressure was on, and soon we were paddling again.

Wolves howled in the night at our camp east of Meadow Portage, reminding us that we were still in the wilderness of the three big lakes, Winnipeg, Winnipegosis and Manitoba, the residues of glacial Lake Agassiz. This lightly populated land — too heavily treed for big grain farms, too isolated for big industry, too cold for many — possesses a beauty all its own, with clean water, jagged points, sandy bays, birch and aspen bluffs, and all the many denizens of the wild that thrive in such an environment such as deer, moose, mink, beaver and wolf.

But it was people — helpful and trusting people — who again stood out.

By noon on Day 13, Sept. 13, we stopped near Crane River Reserve at the home of Alfred Morrisseau, and I called my parents to congratulate them on their 50th wedding anniversary. (Imagine being happily married, to the same person, for 50 years.) They were glad to hear we were well.

Farther on, at a grassy island, Athena chased frogs. She was better. My thumb remained sore and stiff. (Eventually the nail fell off, revealing a new one underneath.) That evening the winds that dogged us almost daily continued, and we were driven ashore, broadsided by breakers that soaked us and then dropped us on rocks. Cows watched bemusedly and chewed their cud as we unpacked. Meanwhile, Athena went AWOL and was gone for the night.

Where were the prevailing westerly winds? It had been a week since we'd had a friendly wind and we were fed up fighting headwinds. If this was God's way of testing our resolve, as Mark figured it was, it was a long test. Mark and I both believed in God, in a higher power, and this trip both challenged and confirmed our faith. Mark, for one, was reading the Bible each day--not secondary texts about the Bible, just the good book itself. Next day, Sept. 14, rain pelted our tent as we awoke, the wind howled, and we stayed put. God gave us good sense and normally we followed it.

❦

As morning broke we heard a loud "Meow!" and then Athena jumped into the back of the tent. We got her inside and she slept and dried off in my bag. I was pretty pleased to have her back.

Soon we had a visitor from the farmhouse 250 metres away. He thought we were lost.

"Where are you from?" asked the farmer. Mark explained.

"You canoed all this way?" Then I asked if he planned to watch the Canada-U.S. hockey game that night.

"No, I'm going to bingo," said the man, who was in his 50s. "Do you want to watch the game? I'll leave the house unlocked for you."

"Fantastic," we said.

"If it rains, you can sleep there too."

We watched the game and returned to the tent, never to see our friend again. We left him some fruit.

Next day was a banner day, as we did about 64 kilometres. We were then about 500 kilometres from The Pas. A strong northwest wind was just what we needed to escape from that fly-infested cow pasture. It was getting crazy, what with a zillion flies in our tent. We'd open the flap just to let them out!

We were elated to reach the Lake Manitoba Narrows, west of Ashern, where we went under a bridge on Highway 68. We made some thrilling crossings that day, one a 16-kilometre stretch that tested us well, but Jimmy-Jock was extremely seaworthy. Those big lakes were shallow, with numerous reefs that were dangerous even to us. So far we'd hit only one rock a glancing blow. Our stomachs were a bit upset, as we had eaten boiled dandelions tainted by manure from the pasture. We didn't do that again. We sailed a lot, saving our energy.

By the way, we navigated the lakes by a Manitoba Highways map. And we didn't feel a need for anything more.

Another 40 kilometres on Sept. 16 put us just north of Sandy Bay Reserve on the lake's west side. At 6:15 p.m., near shore in shallow water, something strange happened. The wind abated somewhat, and we were suddenly clobbered by a wave that seemed to come from nowhere. It caught us completely off guard and dumped buckets of water upon us. Mark was as stunned as I was. Our closest call yet. Earlier that day we spotted what we think was a fox — on an island. Do foxes swim? They must.

Another gale blew in on us, halting our progress. Mark finished *Captains Courageous* and was then reading *Kon-Tiki*, the great true story of a voyage by raft from Peru to the Polynesian Islands. I greatly enjoyed Homer's *Odyssey*.

The morning of Sept. 18 we awoke to find a skiff of snow on the ground. It was -1 C. Our first snow.

☙

I went out for a long walk with the shotgun to try to bag a duck or goose, when nature called. I'd seen no birds to that point. Then, with my pants around my ankles and the gun against a tree, a small flock of geese flew over, within easy range. Oh well. You might say they were saved by the smell.

Mark and I spent part of the day by the fire, drying our clothes. We got wet and cold, but our health was good. Another day and we'd be off this blasted big lake. Lake Manitoba was a real challenge, especially the portion south of the Narrows. We figured it was the most dangerous portion of all the big lakes we paddled, including Cedar and Winnipegosis, because of its shallow rocky shorelines, hidden shoals and unpredictable winds. Sometimes we had to paddle furiously to avoid being carried out into the middle. I was glad to see the end of that cursed lake, and I know Mark shared my sentiments.

RUSS MEAD AND KAREN CONVERY

We arrived at the Delta Marsh Field Station on Sept. 19, marking the end of our journey on Lake Manitoba. We were met by the station's manager, Russ Mead, a 39-year-old scientist. He told us we were the first canoeists to come down the lake since he started there in 1985. The bearded Mead served us hot chocolate. Then Karen Convery brought us soup and sandwiches. So helpful. We also had a shower in their '30s-era lodge.

The research station did work in the areas of ornithology and marsh life and was then part of the University of Manitoba. After a couple of hours we continued on, heading up the floodway after a short portage. Wilf Monkman, who had helped with our sail, had told me about the two large concrete abutments he had helped construct there years ago, so we couldn't miss it.

For the first time, Athena fell in the water. I accidentally knocked her off with my arm as she crawled around me. She sure swam well. And she had such a look of determination on her face as she cat-paddled to the canoe. We'd gone a good six metres before we could stop and back up. I reached down to grab her but she spurned my offer of help and got in by herself. At least she was clean after her dip, and seemed quite pleased with her Mark Spitz imitation.

The floodway soon became a nightmare for us. It had enough water, but in places was choked with cattails and bulrushes. We hauled the canoe through the thick of it, feeling like Humphrey Bogart in *The African Queen*. By 8 the sun was down, but we were far from clear. The creek was as choked as ever. We'd hauled Jimmy-Jock about five kilometres, taking turns like horses. While one of us wore a rope around our chest, the other pushed with a paddle along the shore. It was exhausting and depressing work. That night things froze, and some of our stuff was wet. The morning of the 20th I flagged down a guy with a pickup, Ron Moffat, and he took us to the Assiniboine River a short distance away.

We needed supplies — boots, sleeping bag, snowsuits. We also lacked a frying pan, but decided to do without. We'd left ours back at Wooden Tent, the first stop. We cooked out of a large pickle can. In it we made soups and boiled fish and foil dinners. It's all we needed. We baked fish in tin foil, too. Beans were eaten cold from the can. We ate tinned salmon, tuna, noodles, granola bars, apples, bananas, raisins and nuts, and chokecherries whenever possible. We ate well. Along the Assiniboine we were close to fields of carrots, potatoes and parsnips, where remnants from the harvest remained for us to use.

On Sept. 20 we carried around the fourth and final dam on the Assiniboine River. But the cat went AWOL again in the afternoon, forcing us to wait the night. Losing four hours of good paddling time had us both downcast. The race against oncoming winter was still on, and we had a long way to go. I wasn't looking forward to paddling 400 miles or 643 kilometres against the current on the Red River. On the bright side, a man named Robbie, from Natural Resources, gave me a ride into town and I bought the gear we needed. Each night now dipped below freezing.

The cat came back, and we were away early the next day, Sept. 22, when we were on the water for 14½ long hours. The previous night we unknowingly camped in a low spot, and got soaked during an all-night rain. All the more reason to push it and reach the home of Mark's aunt and uncle, Doreen and Elmer Giesbrecht, in Winnipeg that night.

We were kindly treated by Ron and Leslie Unruh, who lived near Elie, a small community west of Winnipeg. They had a beautiful spread near the river. We were awed by their affluence — pool, horses, beautiful grounds. Like many on the city's outskirts, they commuted to Winnipeg for work.

In another brief encounter a nice lady gave us two tomatoes for lunch. We would stop for five or 10 minutes for water or to check about food, when we were low. "You're not dressed warmly enough!" she admonished.

"We stay warm paddling," I replied. We wore jogging pants, boots, sweatshirts and jackets. It was a few degrees above freezing, and drizzling.

The Assiniboine meandered crazily, doubling back on itself, as we searched for the Perimeter bridge, where Mark's uncle would pick us up. By 10:30 p.m. we were still on the water, paddling by moonlight. I was exhausted, and wanted to stop to phone him from a house, but Mark was determined to keep going to the rendezvous point by the bridge. We saw many flocks of geese settled for the night, and heard their calls of alarm. We also saw many beavers working in the moonlight, an incredible number. We almost rammed some of them. There were so many tails slapping the water that it sounded like a war zone.

Athena was funny that night as we paddled. She'd stick her head out of the splash cover and look at me as if to say, "Are you guys still paddling? C'mon, we need to get to bed!"

Finally, at 11:15 p.m., we reached the bridge and saw Elmer. That day we did 80 incredible kilometres, most of it in a cold rain. We had made it to the city in three weeks, some 765 kilometres from The Pas. We remained determined to reach New Orleans by Dec. 15.

"Are you hungry, boys?" his aunt asked. Our reply was to eat vast quantities of Doreen's cabbage rolls, mashed potatoes and apple pie, as she,

Elmer and their son Doug watched in amazement. We slept the dreamless sleep of the exhausted.

Next day, while Mark and I picked up some supplies, Elmer repaired our seat webbing. He also gave us a new watertight pail for our cameras and other valuables.

Mark and I were mailing some letters in a Winnipeg drugstore when who should I find in line ahead of me but Bert Aconley, an uncle I hadn't seen in years. "Uncle Bert, it's you!" We had a good reunion. I got his address and so began a relationship with my mother's only brother that remained strong until he died on Christmas Day, 2001, at 87. Without this trip, I likely would never have rekindled a relationship with the man, and would have been the poorer for it. He taught me, for instance, that I spent too much time reading and not enough time getting things done. The fact this book is written is a credit to him.

I decided to leave Athena in Winnipeg. A friend from The Pas, Vicki Hornick, drove down to get her. There was too much risk of dogs and rain and snow from there on, and she would just have been in the way and miserable.

We were set to begin the second leg of our journey, 725 kilometres to Minneapolis via the Red and Minnesota Rivers. The Pas to Winnipeg was our shakedown cruise. After adding some new gear and leaving some behind, we felt confident of achieving our next goal.

We left Winnipeg Sept. 24 from the point at which we arrived, and 90 minutes later were at the Forks, amazed by its development. It boasted a market and many stores. That was fitting, as for thousands of years the confluence of the Red and Assiniboine rivers had been a meeting place for Aboriginal peoples such as the Cree and Assiniboine. There they traded, celebrated, and sometimes fought. The young met and married; the old relived their heydays. Winnipeg originated there as the Red River Settlement, begun in 1812 when a Scottish philanthropist brought in poor farmers to settle the area, via the Hayes River and York Factory. By the later 1800s river boats were in use, ferrying goods from North Dakota and Minnesota north and foodstuffs south. The forks had been an ancient meeting place, a hub of the fur trade, the site of the first farming settlement in Western Canada, and it remains a centre of commerce today.

The force of the Red's current impressed us, and we knew the coming weeks wouldn't be easy. That, as it turned out, was an understatement.

CHAPTER 7

ARRESTED ON THE RED

It was a good thing I'd left Athena behind, as our first morning without her we were welcomed at the tent by two big dogs. One took off with Mark's mitt, but he got it back. Better the mitt than my cat.

Our outfit now included a canvas tent. Canvas breathes better than nylon, and so our problem with dripping condensation was much reduced. We also now had two air mattresses, eliminating the aching-joints-in-the-morning problem; double sleeping bags, ending the frozen-Brad-and-Mark problem; and a new paddle for Mark. Despite rain the night before we stayed dry, and I hoped my 12-year-old Woods tent would hold out for the duration.

Our first full day on the Red was OK. A strong northwest wind blew us south, and at times, with the sail up, we really flew. It rained a little, and we saw a big buck with a fine rack, as well as two does and a fox. Supper was farmer sausages on sticks over a fire, with cheese, lettuce and cucumbers on bread.

We met a lady suspended over the river with a device that measured water flow. Her name was Annette, and she was pretty. "Are you the guys with the cat? I read about you in the Free Press yesterday."

We admitted to being the party, now catless.

She told us the river was the highest it had been in four years, though still lower than the 100-year average. This was good news: high enough to float us over rocks, low enough to make the current bearable. It soon became very hard going, however. Without a tailwind, we struggled. A normal day saw us paddle from 8 a.m. to 6:30 p.m., stopping only half an hour for lunch, and making maybe 15 miles or 24 kilometres.

On our fourth day south of Winnipeg we approached the United States. The U.S. border was not identified from the Red River. There was no sign and no marker indicating you were entering another country, presumably because long-distance travel by canoe or steamboat went out of fashion about 100 years ago. So, that Saturday evening, Sept. 28, we innocently crossed into the land of the Stars and Stripes. By the time we realized where we were, it was late and dark and we were beat. "We'll phone customs tomorrow," we decided. Well, we didn't do that, fearing they'd boot us off our nice campsite, and rain was threatening. We rested and figured a phone call Monday would be fine. We figured wrong.

"A GUY HERE FROM CANADA"

I called Monday morning at 8. Actually a man from the water treatment plant phoned for us. "Yeah, Jim? There's a guy here from Canada. He and a friend are traveling by canoe. Yeah, canoe."

He handed me the phone and I spoke to Mr. James Gilmore, a border agent who drove out to our camp. "When did you cross the border?" he quietly asked, looking at our tent.

"Saturday night," I told him.

"You're under arrest for illegal entry. You and your friend will have to come back to the office to fill out some forms and answer some questions." There wouldn't have been a problem if we had called Sunday, because you were allowed some lag time.

At the customs office we found out how to get free in the land of the free. First we were questioned in separate rooms about our purpose for being in the U.S. That was pretty simple — we wanted to travel the Mississippi and get to New Orleans. After that, we waited — and Mark was told sharply by another official to sit down when he rose to get a pamphlet from a display case. "You're under arrest!" Then we signed a form admitting we were illegal aliens (I felt like an unwanted Martian), and were deported. That meant walking the 100 metres to the Canadian side, and then back into the U.S., where Mr. Gilmore gave us a ride back to our camp and wished us well. He was very nice throughout.

I treated Mark to steak and eggs ($4.99) to try to cheer him up, and it was good. Finally on the water at 11, we soon returned to our normal rhythm. We saw so many deer we lost count. They clearly were not expecting anyone in a canoe either, and looked just as surprised at our presence as Mr. Gilmore had.

Oct. 1, one month into the trip, was a milestone. We had come about 1,000 kilometres and were adjusting to the Red. We camped near Drayton. The river is the border between Minnesota and North Dakota, which prompted us to joke, "Shall we eat (or camp, or take a break) in North Dakota or Minnesota today?"

"Minnesota — more grass, less gumbo, and no nuclear missiles."

Oh, and no arrests that day. No stores, either. The towns were few and far between and we were running out of food and water, necessitating trips over the banks to farmhouses, where we offered money for food. Just north of Oslo, Minn., Mark went for supplies (we took turns) and came back loaded. "You won't believe what I've got!" he announced as he scrambled over the bank. An elderly lady, Mrs. McGuire, had given him four tins of soup, a tin of veggies, a homemade loaf of bread and a fresh yellow cake — for one dollar. She refused anything more. We inhaled most of the cake at once.

WE DISAGREE

A miserable evening. No decent places to camp. High, muddy banks. We disagreed about what to do; I saw no point in stopping and favoured going on in the moonlight, while Mark wanted to stop, as it was getting dark and we were beat. We compromised and stopped a short while later in a straw-stubble field and put up the wet tent. We faced our share of disagreements, as you might expect when two people are tied to the umbilical cord of a canoe. Sometimes we just didn't talk much. We were stressed because of the lateness in the year, and our bodies and minds were tired from paddling. Fortunately we usually agreed on a course of action, or Mark or I would compromise to suit the other. Luckily for two men who really didn't know each other very well at the start, we got along quite well.

We learned a good cooking lesson: it's not wise to make tea from macaroni water, especially when the tea bag is used and three days old. On the bright side, we found we were gaining on the sun. There was light still at 7:30 p.m. The weather was warmer, but the Red River gumbo was brutal. We could hardly walk at times because of the mud on our boots.

ೞ

On Oct. 2 we again needed food, so I went up to a place called Robbin and went from house to house. We hadn't seen a store in days. One man and his wife, who were newcomers from Central America, insisted I take some food and refused money. Theirs was the most humble of the homes I went to, but they helped me most. A well-dressed lady gave me a loaf of bread for my proffered dollar.

By 3:30 on Oct. 4 our spirits were low and our jokes pretty limp. Where in the world was Oslo? (In Europe.) We had hoped to get there the day before. We needed a store! It was cold (-5 C) and we required lots of food to stay warm and paddle hard.

"Do you smell something?" Mark asked, in accordance with our joke about smelling bridges before we saw them.

"I do indeed." Finally, the Oslo bridge. We came to like bridges, for they signified towns, and seeing that bridge did wonders for our spirits.

Getting to Oslo was a huge relief. Gigantic. It took so long to get there. We were tired of paddling east and west — more than south — along that blasted meandering river. What took 16 kilometres by car took three times the distance by canoe, and that's a fact. That was roughly the ratio all the way south on the Red. It was brutal and I've often said I'd never paddle it again unless very well paid. We, of course, were doing it for nothing.

Priority No. 1 was groceries. While Mark stayed with Jimmy-Jock, I found a store and bought $52 worth of food, filling two boxes and two bags. "Load me up!" I told the clerks. "These arms have paddled a canoe from Canada; they can certainly carry this." On my way back to the river a man named Max Campbell stopped to give me a ride. Mr. Campbell also let us use his shower, and so we cleaned up for the first time in 10 days. He told us the river straightened out from there on, cheery news.

Mark and I roasted Polish sausages over a fire on sticks that night.

Our money was holding out well. My weekly articles were appearing in the Opasquia Times, which kept some cash flowing. And I'd saved enough to buy food and a used car to carry us home. I've never worried much about money, even less so when I hardly had any, such as during this period.

Next day we reached Grand Forks, population 44,000. On Oct. 7, just before we left the city, we met Jeff, who told us the next part of the river we'd paddle, the Bois de Sioux, had water in it, the first time in four years! "You guys sure picked the right time to do this trip," said our bearded friend. "You know, not many guys do what you're doing anymore. You're a dying breed."

We busily broke camp and packed the canoe as he talked. "Hey, did you guys see many clams on the Assiniboine River? My brothers and I take five to 10 tons of clams a year."

"For what? Meat?"

"No, the shells. The shells are a dollar a pound." I'd never heard of clam picking.

Jeff also said our next big city, Fargo, was 180 miles or 290 kilometres away, with six dams to get around.

After six hours paddling we made 40 kilometres. I wrenched my back, but it seemed OK. This would come up later on, however. By 7:30 it was getting dark as we sat by our fire. "Whoo, whoo, whoo" called an owl. But for that, a breeze in the trees and the sizzle of our fire, it was quiet.

Next day we hit long shallow stretches of fast water, slowing us down. Once or twice we got out and pulled. Another farm woman gave us water and a loaf of bread, refusing our money. "I wish my son was here," she said. "He'd be so interested. Listen, it's easy to catch catfish. Just find a frog and soon you'll have a two-foot catfish! My son does that."

"Sounds good. Thanks." We never did. Couldn't do that to a frog.

౿∂౿

We found a floating pumpkin and cooked it. We also ate strips of it raw. At Halstead we got more groceries, and more ice cream. We called ourselves the ice cream-powered paddlers. The grocer wanted $24 for a fishing licence, so we declined.

That night we camped on a game trail and I joked to Mark that I hoped the deer looked before they leapt. Next morning, two deer did come bounding toward us. The leading one hit the brakes at the last moment, and our eyes met. He looked shocked. That deer honestly had a shocked look on its face. He was big, too, with a small rack. They turned and high-tailed it out of there.

DESERTED AND MOODY

A few days later it was my turn to get water, so up the bank I went to a farm. Saturday morning, 9:30, somewhere in North Dakota. I didn't like the feel of the place from the start. It felt deserted and moody. There were two houses and a machine shed; a truck and a three-wheeler were parked nearby.

I knocked hesitantly at one of the homes. No answer. At the house beside it I knocked again and a woman in her 40s opened the door, her face hard. When I said "please" in asking for water, she softened. "There's a tap around the back, help yourself."

In fact there were two taps, hot and cold. The woman appeared at the patio door a few metres away. A thermometer on the wall read 42 F.

"Where are you from?" she asked as I filled our two-litre soft drink containers.

"Canada. A place called The Pas, in Manitoba. We've come more than 800 miles," I said proudly. "This is our 42nd day."

"How do you stay warm?"

"Paddling keeps us warm. At night we have double sleeping bags and snow suits."

"And you're going to New Orleans. Won't the river freeze up?"

"No, the current's too fast. Once we hit the Minnesota River we're laughing. Do you know how far it is from here?"

"No."

I finished filling our jugs. "Ma'am, I noticed some squash at the front of your house. Would you mind if we had one, I mean, took one to eat?"

"Go ahead, I'll see you at the front." She appeared there a minute later with a bag of onions and some carrots for us too.

"These cherry tomatoes wasting in the dirt, could I grab some?" She said yes, and I explained our need for fresh food, and lots of it, to keep ourselves fueled.

As I squatted for the tomatoes, I heard a man's gruff voice. "Do you have any ID? What's your name?"

I stood up to my full 6-2 height and looked down on a slim, weather-worn farmer in his late 40s.

"My name's Brad. Brad Bird. I have no ID on me," I said, looking him in the eye. He was afraid. My large sheath knife hung handily at my waist, and I was in no mood to undergo an inquisition. Never am, actually.

"We're having a problem with theft," he said. "The other day the wife and I leave for two hours to attend a wedding, and when we get back one of our three-wheelers is gone."

"Well, I'm sorry to hear that, but don't look at me. I'm traveling by canoe from Manitoba to New Orleans, and I've never been here before. I just came up for water."

"Upriver?"

"Yes, we're paddling upriver. We've come about 400 miles from Winnipeg. And it's brutal at times, awful."

"I know," he said. "Last year a friend and I went five miles upriver and it took half a day. Listen, I'm sorry about coming on so strong."

"Don't mention it. I understand, and me looking like this, dressed like this. There's a big problem with theft back home, too."

We walked toward the dike and canoe, chatting some more, relaxed now. "Hey, do you want your squash?" the woman said.

"Sure do," I said, smiling, and went back for it.

"Why are you doing this?" she asked.

"For adventure. I get bored at a desk. I like to be moving, I like to be free. Listen, my friend is waiting. Thanks for the water and stuff. Nice talking to you." It was getting pretty personal and emotional I wanted to leave.

"Nice meeting you," she said, as the man stood near her. He had come from the first house. He hadn't answered the door, and I'm not sure why. Suspicion or fear, maybe. When a three-wheeler disappears, so does a certain amount of trust.

STABBING LOWER BACK PAIN

Some days later, at Grand Forks, my back went out. I couldn't walk or bend. Lying flat on my back was the least painful position. For a while it looked like our trip might even be over — an awful prospect, unthinkable. Sleep was next to impossible as knives of pain stabbed my lower back when I made the slightest movement. Turning over was out of the question.

That morning, I told Mark the bad news: "Maybe I've slipped a disc." He said a prayer, simple and direct, and my back got better — rapidly. The next day we moved on. I still felt pressure on my spine, but that day something clicked back into place, and the pain relented. It was gone completely within days.

Twice now, Mark had prayed for my recovery — the other time was when I ate poisonous berries — and recovery was swift. Coincidence? I don't think so.

We happened by Wahpeton, a town of 10,000, on Homecoming Weekend and saw quite a parade. Mark was approached by a lady who told him she was "pushing 90."

"Where are you from?" she asked him.

"Canada." Then she pressed two candies into his hand and took him over to some friends. "This boy's from Canada." She also wanted to give him money and buy him a burger, but he declined. She was pretty impressed that he'd canoed from Canada.

At Wahpeton the river narrowed and changed names. It was now the Bois de Sioux. This was where the Ottertail River flowed into it, and this was the start of the Red River of the North. There is also a Red River in the American South.

At a pizza joint one evening we were interviewed by a local reporter. Two rather pretty young women showed us some welcome attention. They would have liked to have spent more time with us and, frankly, I wouldn't have minded. But we had to move on.

Mark mentioned that he dreamed a lot more than he did at home. He slept lighter outdoors, while I slept deeper. I also dreamt a lot more, having incredibly vivid dreams with people from my past. An example: I was working at a North Dakota nuclear missile station and my monitor showed the Russians had launched an attack. Awful. I reported to our commander, who was Al Yaskiw, school superintendent in The Pas, a contact in my reporting days. He tried to call the president and then, thankfully, I woke up.

The day after Wahpeton, Oct. 20, we reached the 1,000-mile mark (1,600 kilometres). It was our 50th day, so we were averaging 32 kilometres a day. The next 3,200 kilometres to New Orleans we expected to be easier, as it was mostly with the current.

The landscape changed. Until then you could be plunked down on the Red at Fargo, N.D. or Morris, Man. and not know the difference. On the Bois de Sioux there were far fewer trees and sandier soil. The river was also much straighter. We crossed a few beaver dams, and lodged in one of them was a big sucker, still alive. We cooked and ate it.

At the White Rock Dam we left the upstream paddling behind, and looked out over a reservoir, Lake Traverse. As we moved our gear over to the Traverse side, a man in a pickup drove up. "Are you the guys canoeing from Canada? I'm a game warden, and I'd like to talk to you."

Game Warden Marty Stage wasn't looking to hassle us but help us. And he wanted to know all about our adventure. Since that would take some time, he invited us to his home. First, though, we had to paddle another

35 kilometres across Lake Traverse to Brown's Valley, where he would pick us up.

Could we do it? He gave us three ducks to eat, and we quickly "breasted" them, and then left around 1. We got to Brown's Valley at 7:15. It was a breeze to paddle on a lake again. (By the way, we paddled shirtless that day, and we understand it snowed in The Pas. We were not as crazy as some people thought!)

We hid the canoe in the trees and carried our laundry and sleeping bags into town. It felt good to walk. We strode down the middle of Minnesota State Highway 27 in the moonlight without a care in the world. We felt like kings and talked like it too. In town we bought submarine sandwiches and phoned Marty. While we waited, a patrolman drove up and asked us what we were doing, and we explained. We must have looked suspicious, dressed shabbily as we were and waiting on a street corner for Marty.

At his home we were served lasagna by his wife, Jinny. They told us how much they had been helped by others on trips, which is why they tried to help travelers when possible. We did a wash and chatted with them well into the night.

Next morning, after only five hours' sleep, Marty drove us back to the canoe with his pickup, and we loaded our gear. It was a bit of a drive to Big Stone Lake, over the continental divide. Water on the south side flowed into the Mississippi; on the north side it flowed to Hudson Bay. Mark said he felt a bit guilty as we passed the clogged creek that Don Starkell and his boys, whom I mentioned earlier, had struggled on. I didn't share his sentiment. We'd struggled enough, and were making no claim to paddling every inch of the way. Besides, if we didn't make tracks south quickly, freeze-up would end our trip.

After a full day's paddle we reached Ortonville, where we collected fresh supplies. The highlight of the day was Mark's duck soup. It tasted great.

Next day we finally got on the Minnesota River, which began as a winding narrow creek. Many fallen trees blocked our advance, forcing us over and under them. Finally, on Marsh Lake, we saw thousands of geese.

LAC QUE DE PARLE

On Lac Que de Parle, another reservoir, we spotted something on the water. It was a floating dead goose, which we quickly named Sam. Just before this we had been on the wrong channel, headed for the wrong river, when we saw two men on shore. We hadn't seen anyone for hours. Was a higher power helping us again? The men told us we needed to backtrack and go around the point, so we did. That's where we found Sam. He tasted great too. We roasted his big drumsticks, which dripped juice and fat. That and a stew made for a feast.

That morning we came across two hunters, dressed like Rambo, a movie figure who wages war single-handedly. I think we intruded on their fantasy. "How far to Lac qui Parle?" we asked.

"Two miles to the bridge, and another two after that. You mean you're going all the way to Lac qui Parle?"

Was he serious? He couldn't have been. "Yes" was all we said.

On Oct. 25 we had to change a flat tire. We hit a rock in some fast water and cracked Jimmy-Jock a short gash, which leaked. We emptied him, started a fire, dried the affected area and patched him with resin and fibreglass. Our repair kit was big enough to fix major damage, if need be. We lost three hours.

At Montevideo we mailed letters and got supplies. Maple trees were more common there, and so were apple orchards. Next day, Oct. 26, around kilometer 1,900 of the trip, we saw a man picking up windfall apples in his backyard at Granite Falls. If there's one thing Mark and I truly savoured, it was those great Minnesota apples. "You can't buy any, but I'll give you some," Gerry Baker told us as we paddled close. And so began a pleasant visit. In his early 60s, Mr. Baker tended his four trees with great care, and stored his produce in a fruit cellar at the side of the house he had built 27 years earlier. He gathered a dozen big Cortland apples (which don't turn brown after you bite or bake them).

"Mary, we've got a couple of canoeists from Canada," he announced. His wife wanted to know where we were from. At their request, I sketched our route on their map. "Well I'll be," she said, and then gave us a bag with carrot cake and bread. "We've got four boys, and they'll be interested to hear about what you're doing," Gerry said. We returned to the canoe, where the couple met Mark, who had wanted to stay behind.

A little farther on we portaged around another dam and then saw a man on a rocky shore. Yes, it was Mr. Baker. "Forgot to get your picture," he said, snapping a couple off. "You be sure to write when you get home." I did.

CHAPTER 8

STORM OF THE CENTURY

On Oct. 29 the temperature fell, and the next day it began to snow. Normally we caught the weather forecast each morning on our little radio, but didn't on Oct. 30 for some reason. Not that it would have made much difference. We had to paddle, rain or snow. At New Ulm we picked up some supplies and visited the town three times because the river meandered so much.

The next day, Halloween, the snow became serious at Mankato. We stopped at 10 a.m. to make a fire and warm our frigid feet. The snow began to fall with a fury and didn't abate. Soon the landscape was white. We made soup and plenty of sandwiches, bagging them for supper in case a fire later wasn't possible.

We paddled into a light wind, but didn't think much of it. After all, how bad could an early storm be? Pretty bad, we found out. It would go down in local annals as the Halloween Blizzard of '91, the "Storm of the Century," a three-day blast that would dump 70 centimetres of snow on southern Minnesota.

By 2 p.m. the storm had intensified and we knew we had to be careful. The next town was about three hours distant, and we saw no houses or buildings of any sort. At 3 we decided to stop at a sheltered curve in the river. As I struggled to get a fire going, Mark put up the tent. We ate lots — two boxes of macaroni, beans, mackerel and bread, saving our sandwiches for later.

Drying clothes was a losing battle in the pelting wet snow, so we escaped to the tent, only to have to get out an hour later when it collapsed.

The two end pegs that held up the poles were forced out by the weight of the white stuff on the canvas. I cut new pegs from saplings, as the original ones were buried.

They held and we slept as the wind howled. Waking up from time to time, I hit the roof to remove snow. We were warm enough even without our snow suits, which were wet. Everything was wet. It was -2 C. By morning the tent roof was almost touching our faces, it was so heavily laden. Forty centimetres had fallen and the storm was intense. This time we had the radio on, and the announcer said a lot more snow was expected and the temperature was to fall to 5 F two days hence. That's about -15 C, very cold. So there would be no reprieve. We decided to paddle toward the next town, as there seemed no advantage to waiting and freezing where we were. Paddling, at least, kept us warm.

The next scene was right out of a British TV comedy. We had quite a few laughs. "How to fold a tent in the snow," we joked, taking on English accents. "First, leave everything in the bloody tent." We did, too. Why take it out? "Next, throw the corners into the centre and roll it up in one big mess." That's what it was.

The canoe, of course, was buried. Brushing off what we could, we tossed the tent onto Jimmy-Jock and shoveled out places to sit. We'd torn the old tent in taking it down, as it was frozen to the ground in places, but the tear wasn't serious. Hoping we'd left nothing behind, we headed out. Fortunately we got some great photos of the snow with my Pentax K-1000.

A POLAR LANDSCAPE

The snow drove into us like sand, stinging our eyes. That's what I remember most, the sore eyes. We still had to watch for deadheads and other obstacles, and that's tough when you're squinting, and not wearing glasses, in which state I'm half blind. My glasses got snowed up and fogged up in minutes, so they came off. But we were able to make pretty good time, and we noticed a certain beauty in the landscape. Everything was starkly white, like a polar landscape. We chatted and joked and made the best of it.

Heads down, backs bent, we paddled vigorously. Near 10 a.m. we saw a bridge; the town was close. We pulled up under the bridge and walked through knee-deep snow into Le Sueur. Along the way we pushed a

Cadillac out of a low spot and bought a couple of long johns at a bake shop. Feeling better, we continued down the street to the only motel, where we got the last room.

That evening, Nov. 1, a Friday, we were interviewed in our room by Bill Floyd, editor of the *Le Sueur News-Herald*. Bill was easy to talk to, and we ended up making the front page of the Nov. 6 edition. His lead was, "In the middle of a major snowstorm, one has to think the Minnesota River isn't the ideal place to be spending your time. But that's where two Canadians found themselves last Friday morning."

By next morning 71 centimetres had fallen. We retrieved the tent and sleeping bags to dry them, and checked the canoe, which we'd stashed under the bridge. All was well. We wanted to be moving, as we were only 97 kilometres from the Mississippi. But it was cold, and the river was freezing up. We didn't want to be stuck there, but the choice was out of our hands. After church on Sunday, a man named Bruce Steinke gave us a hand by moving our gear in his truck back to the river. He also paid for our motel room, for which we were grateful. Our budget didn't include hotel rooms. In traveler's cheques and cash, I started with about $2,500 US. That had to buy a used car in New Orleans, as well as food and gear to get there.

We got on the river and broke ice with our paddles, but it became too thick to break after an hour or so. We didn't want to go back and be defeated. For as long as we could, we broke ice and plodded on, but it was getting colder, the ice thicker.

"I feel like fighting on," Mark said. So did I. For a while longer we struggled to make a short distance. Then we came upon a large ice jam, and Mark got out and walked around a corner to see its extent. "A quarter-mile, anyway."

The temperature had fallen to -8 C. It was 3:30, and the day was getting colder. "Maybe we could rig a harness and pull it along the bank," he suggested.

"She's pretty steep and treacherous," I replied. "And the trees are thick. Plus, there's two feet of snow and we could slip into the river."

"Maybe we should pray about this," he suggested. We did. Then, disappointed, we turned back.

Next day, Nov. 4, we got a ride into Minneapolis with a man we had met at the bakeshop. We rented a car for $90, which took us to Dubuque,

Iowa, 400 kilometres south of Minneapolis. But that wasn't the last of the snow.

                           ৡৈ

We first glimpsed the mighty Mississippi at 2:10 a.m. on Nov. 5th, and it was a special moment. Even in the middle of the night we sensed the power and majesty of the river as it glided by in the lights of the city. We heard the buzz of industry around it, felt the energy of the river even at that hour, and knew we were about to embark on something special. The word *Mississippi* comes from the Ojibwa name "Messipi," which means *great river*. The Algonquin called it *Missi Sepe*, "great river," or, poetically, "father of waters." At 2,320 miles (3,733 kilometres) the Mississippi is the longest river in the United States. A leaf falling in Lake Itasca, its source in Minnesota would arrive at the Gulf of Mexico in about 90 days. We had joined the great river about a third of its way down. Thinking about the adventure to come, we settled back in the car for sleep.

At 3:10 a.m. a flashlight was shone in our eyes. As I came awake I saw a uniformed man with a light. Rolling down the window, I told him we were trying to sleep.

"I can see that," the policeman replied, unimpressed. We told our story about the rented Lumina, the ice farther north and our trip to New Orleans. He frowned. "It's cold down here, too."

"Yeah, but there's no snow. We can take the cold without the snow." He left. One hundred communities from North Dakota to the State of Mississippi set records for cold temperatures the previous day. We couldn't outrun it.

Dubuque, Iowa, was named for a French-Canadian fur trader, just as Le Sueur had been. At 6 a.m., semi-trailers began to stream into our parking lot at Dubuque and we awoke and returned the car. Then the moment we had been waiting for — we launched the canoe on the river. As soon as the current embraced us we knew this ride would be different. After two hours on the big river we were wet; it was snowing. But it felt great to be on the Mississippi at last. The first barges we saw were immense compared to our frail craft, but we were making good time. And we felt safe.

Distance on the Mississippi is measured in miles, and the markers are clearly and frequently displayed on shore. Next day, despite two long stops to buy mitts and dry some clothes, we paddled 35 miles (56 kilometres). The current pushed us along at about three m.p.h.

We camped that night just north of Bellevue, and the temperature fell to -11 C.

At Bellevue we passed through our first of many locks and dams. These structures reduce the risk of flooding and keep river levels high for commercial traffic. You wait in line with other boats, enter the lock, which fills up with water like a bathtub, and a door opens at the other end to send you on your way. We met a Corps of Engineers man there who didn't like our chances. "Do you know that a person freezes to death in 30 seconds in this water?" he said. He also said the 37-mile stretch to Lock No. 13 was the most dangerous on the river — prophetic words as it turned out, but we didn't appreciate them. We had found the first four-fifths of that stretch easy. Heck, the big Manitoba lakes had been more challenging. We should have known better, because almost every bit of water we had traveled surprised us at the end. But we were cocky. Hey, we had paddled from The Pas!

CRAZY MEN ON THE RIVER

At Sabula, where we stopped for some shopping, a grocer named Mr. Ackerman said he'd heard about us — the "two crazy men paddling the river." We assured him we were sane, but maybe deluded.

After drying everything in a Laundromat at Sabula — even our tent, which I don't recommend — we camped that night on a lush green island a bit north of Lock and Dam 13 near Clinton. I remember us trying very hard, paddling long and hard in darkness, to reach the dam and get through it, as it would have blocked the passage of some of the ice behind us. Paddling beyond it to the south would surely have been safer, but we didn't quite get there, despite pushing hard.

We went to bed with a clear river only metres away and awoke to quite a different world. "Uh oh, Mark," I said outside the tent, surveying the large plates and chunks of ice that filled the Mississippi early that morning.

"What's the matter?"

"More ice. Lots of it. Even along shore here, there's maybe one place we can safely launch from." That's all there was — one place. The rest of the shoreline was frozen in ice that reached into the river for two or three metres or more.

After discussing the situation we decided to leave before it got so bad we couldn't get away at all. We headed for the west shore, Iowa. The east shore was Illinois. In Iowa we would find a phone and call the Corps people at the dam to learn if it was clear. Well, we got to the shore and found a friendly couple who let us use their phone. But I didn't get through to the dam. An operator said it was long distance to Illinois. I didn't want to run up a bill for the couple whose home we were in. Big mistake.

I phoned an Iowa radio station instead and was told the river south of the dam was clear, but what we needed were the conditions at the dam. Was it even allowing boats through? The radio man didn't know. The homeowner, a decent chap in his early 50s, tried his best to discourage us from leaving, suggesting we camp at the nearby park and wait a day or two. We ignored his good advice. We thanked him and his wife, who had given us some canned meat, and got back on the water. It was as if the true hazards of the ice-clogged river just didn't register with us. Were we blinded by our ambition to keep moving?

The river was choked with ragged pieces of ice, some bigger than table tops. Most were as thick as a laptop computer. In the distance, near the middle, a barge had cut a pathway through, and this illusion became our objective. As we drifted toward the dam, crunching over and through the plates of ice, the laneway disappeared like a desert mirage.

We were moving deceptively fast, but because the floes were moving equally fast with the current we didn't appreciate our pace. All the while Jimmy-Jock went over and through the ice, sometimes pushing it aside. At the start we were confident. Soon we were much less so, often being sandwiched between the plates, unable to set our own course. And it was noisy. The constant grinding and crunching of ice against ice — and ice against fibreglass — told us we had maybe taken on too much.

Soon we saw the lock — it came upon us faster than we expected — and noted it was frozen in by 100 metres or so of backed-up ice. We didn't know until then that the lock and dam were serving as a bottleneck for most of the ice bearing down upon it. It was as if the river we rode was the wide part of a funnel, and the narrow part of the funnel was the lock and dam. Some ice was able to pass through the funnel by falling over the spillway — a three- to four-metre drop beside the lock — but most of it backed up near the east shore and along the lock. They couldn't, or wouldn't, open the lock doors. The only way past the lock was over the spillway, and neither of us felt like swimming. It was sunny and -3 C.

We had to shout to hear ourselves above the din of grinding ice, and by this time we were shouting a fair bit, trying to get out of the mess. Mark or I would point out a gap among the floes, and we would shoot for it against the current, away from the dam. Our goal was to fight our way upstream to a place on shore where we could land, and we made several vigorous attempts. But it was impossible to achieve, as plates of ice bore down upon us, closing the gaps they teasingly opened. We'd get ahead maybe 50 metres and then be carried back even farther by ice.

NO WAY OUT

At that point I realized we were in trouble. There was no way out unless we went over the spillway. For the first time in the trip, we could not control the outcome. We could not control where we went. Because I sat in the back, I could see what the ice was doing to the canoe, scraping it, cutting it, squeezing it with great force. It occurred to me that we might spring a leak.

We paddled like pile drivers. Good thing we were fit. By then a row of cars had lined up along the Illinois shore, the east shore closest to us. The vultures had landed in waiting. At least, that's how I viewed the people gawking at us from their vehicles. At that point we were waiting too. Aware that all we were doing was exhausting ourselves, we slipped alongside the pack ice that sat against the shore and out from the lock. At first we clung to the ice with our mitts.

"I can't hold!" Mark shouted, as oncoming ice lifted the bow and swung us around. For some minutes, we struggled to grip the ice and hold our place, again and again being dislodged.

We ended up in a little haven, an indent along the edge of the ice that allowed most of the oncoming floes to pass us harmlessly by. We smartened up and flung two bungee cords out, hooking one end to the jagged ice and the other to the canoe. This saved a lot of effort.

Minutes later we heard a faint voice over the cacophony of rumbling and grinding floes. "Can't hear you!" I shouted.

Finally the man got off his truck's megaphone and simply yelled to us. "Help is coming in one hour! A tugboat or hovercraft!"

Good news. In the hour we waited we consumed all we could — doughnuts, cookies, milk, water and whatever else we could find to restore our strength. The spillway sat about 100 metres away. We also read. Mark got out his Bible, and I continued a bit with Alistair MacLean's *Puppet on a String*. Each of us said a prayer or two. It was an odd situation, being parked tenuously along pack ice, hoping not to be dislodged and carried over a spillway. I was very much at peace, though. We had logically done everything we could to the best of our ability. Now we were doing the sensible thing by saving our strength. We had reason for hope. I felt strong and relaxed in the stern, comfortable.

In one misguided moment I thought we might be able to walk to shore on the pack ice, but a little pressure from a paddle revealed it was loose and wouldn't support a cat, let alone us. That was close.

Our audience grew as the line of cars lengthened, with onlookers curious to learn our fate. Time ticked by. Ice flowed by. The man was as good as his word, as exactly an hour later we saw it in the lock — a big tug from downstream. This was a regularly scheduled tugboat, but its captain wanted nothing to do with us. I wondered why he sat in the lock for so long, at least 10 minutes. We were told later he had wanted to go straight upriver on his way, without angling over to pluck us from the ice. Had he done this, we would have gone over the spillway for sure as the ice was thrust aside and us with it.

Fortunately Randy Haas and others with the Corps appealed to his sense of decency and convinced him to take a few minutes out of his schedule to pick us up. It may sound corny, but he truly did come in the nick of time. Just as the tug churned through the ice toward us, a massive floe bore down upon us at an angle, sure to dislodge us.

"We've got to get out of here!" I yelled, as Mark peered over his shoulder in alarm. The bow was facing downstream now, toward the dam. Throwing off the bungee cords and driving our paddles into the ice, we shot forward toward the approaching tug.

"Get the hell back!" were the captain's first words over his megaphone. I realize now that his big concern was insurance liability. If we had gone under the tug and drowned, he would have been in a spot of trouble. But we had to move.

"Watch it, Brad!" Mark yelled in response.

"We can't stay here," I said, as the place we sat in moments before was now a picture of vertical ice a metre high forced up by the colliding floes. The tugboat broke through ahead of us.

"Paddle hard for the tug!" the captain yelled, as if we needed encouraging. Big men in one-piece work suits threw us ropes as we pulled alongside. We tossed up some things and then scrambled aboard. They hauled the canoe on deck. We were safe!

"It sure is good to see you guys. Thanks a lot!" I said, and Mark echoed those sentiments.

We never did meet the tug captain, and I'm sorry about that. I would have liked to have thanked him. The fact is he did angle over and pluck us from a bad situation, even if he hadn't wanted to. As it was, the others, including Benny, a six-foot-four giant from Tennessee with an easy smile and a pleasant hillbilly accent, ushered us down to the dining area and gave us coffee. We felt relieved, grateful, and a little ashamed for getting into the fix in the first place. Normally we were more sensible. But this was a new river, a new environment, and we had much to learn. It was humbling.

Later, inside the lock and dam control room, six corpsmen including Mr. Haas marveled at our stamina and manouevres on the river. They had figured we were toast. "Do you guys know you were about four minutes away from meeting your Maker?" one of them said. He also told us he was amazed at the speed we attained in our sallies against the current in an effort to reach an open shore.

We accepted their advice to get off that part of the river and go to St. Louis. "Even Quincey [a town just north of St. Louis] is expecting ice tonight, we're told." We thanked them and did just that, rented another car and drove to St. Louis.

CHAPTER 9

ST. LOUIS AND BEYOND

We arrived in St. Louis at 3 a.m. on Nov. 8 and drove to what looked like a quiet neighbourhood where we intended to sleep until sunrise. But for the second straight time in a rented car, a policeman shone his flashlight on us in the middle of the night. This fellow was nicer than the first.

"How ya doin', partner?" the black man said as I rolled down the window.

"Pretty well," I replied, smiling, and explained our situation. "Is there a problem?"

"You're in a bad neighbourhood. There's crack deals happenin' two blocks away. Chances are your wheels'll be gone by mornin' if ya stayed here. Tell ya what — follow me and I'll show ya a safe place to park and sleep." He did, too, and Mark and I chuckled over that one.

The mercury fell to -12 C even that far south, and we had trouble staying warm in the car. Even in St. Louis, 2,400 kilometres south of The Pas, a thin film of ice formed along a shore of the Mississippi.

All of the newspapers and all of the people we met told us ice-up was four to eight weeks early. This was their coldest November on record. To a large extent we were victims of circumstance, though the trouble at Lock 13 was our own fault. We shouldn't have been on the river. One good thing was that we were sure to be home for Christmas, with all the driving. This was important for Mark, as he had family at home and work lined up for early in the new year. I didn't. Nor was I worried. Worry is a waste, and I figured the future would take care of itself.

REPAIRS TO JIMMY-JOCK

Before we returned the rental car we found a neat little place to camp near the river, up on a bank at an observation point just off a busy road. People would drive in and park for a while to watch the barges go by. There was a patch of grass and trees the size of a typical front lawn beside the parking lot and that's where we put up the tent, cooked our food and repaired the canoe.

Jimmy-Jock had five cuts or breaks in his fiberglass caused by our struggles with ice. Heat hastens the hardening of resin, so I made a small fire. Incredibly, only a thin last layer of fiberglass had kept the water out. The longest gash was 13 centimetres long.

Despite this being a public place in a big city we had privacy and nobody bothered us. Maybe our rough appearances discouraged them. I wore a beard and rough coveralls over a plaid shirt. Mark usually had his cowboy hat on and wasn't much friendlier-looking than I was. Our faces were weather-worn, and no doubt we appeared homeless. Our behaviour, as I look back on it, was that of confident men with a purpose. That alone can be intimidating. One fellow did make a point of talking to us; more about him in a minute.

Besides repairing the canoe that day, we also treated ourselves to a play. We hopped on a bus that took us into downtown St. Louis and saw *Saint Joan* by George Bernard Shaw, as advertised in a newspaper. It was performed by an amateur theatre group in an Anglican church built in 1846. The church featured a huge organ and an extremely high ceiling. One of the actors was introduced as a brain surgeon. The play — what we saw of it — was well done. Unfortunately Mark and I were so tired after our recent river experiences, and after driving through the previous night to get there, that we kept nodding off.

A CURIOUS VISITOR

Next day we were visited by a tall man with a short haircut. His name was Scott. Mark and I wanted someone to take our photo at our campsite, and Scott, in his 30s, was the only one around. So I asked him if he would. We weren't quite prepared for his response.

"Wow, real mountain men!" he exclaimed. "I came by yesterday and saw you working on the canoe, and didn't want to bother you. I'm so glad you talked to me!"

"No problem, Scott." The photo was duly taken. We had to carry our gear down some large rocks and broken concrete blocks to the river's edge. He agreed to help.

"There are so many things I'd like to ask you," he said. "Could I feel your muscles? You must be so strong!" I allowed our friend to touch my bicep. "Wow! It's like concrete!" Mark and I smiled and exchanged glances.

"Just being near you guys, and talking to you, is exciting. I really like your accent." Scott regarded Mark. "How can we get him to talk?"

At that time in his life, aged 19, Mark was not a man to utter 10 words when five would do. And he had said few words in this encounter, beyond something about going to a gas station for a "dump" (which made me chuckle), enough for our visitor to remark, "His accent is so neat!" as if Mark were some kind of alien being, or a special breed of cat.

Then Scott asked: "Could you guys take me with you?" But just as quickly he realized the futility of that request. "Oh, you probably don't have room."

"That's right, Scott, no room. Have you lived in St. Louis long?" I asked, to change the subject.

"All my life. I come to this place to get aluminum cans for recycling. Some people live here for years without knowing about this park. How did you find it?"

"We needed a place handy to the river," and I explained our drive there.

Soon we were packed. We carried Jimmy-Jock carefully down the steep bank and over the large blocks of concrete. He was fixed and watertight again. We eased him into the current and packed our gear aboard, which was a tricky business. But soon we were paddling.

How good it felt to be back on the river! Being forced to drive a car and break the continuity of our trip was unsettling. We lost touch with the river; we lost touch with our lifeline. We both felt that way. It took a day or two on the river to restore our joy and equilibrium and our intimate link with the water.

Maybe there's a bigger message here. Maybe, in some ways, people were better off in the days before cars and planes and trains. Perhaps plodding along at two miles an hour on foot or in Red River carts, or on horseback or paddling in canoes, was better for people than zooming along in automobiles. The old ways allowed you to see nature, feel the wind, watch the birds, chat with fellow travelers, stop any time to enjoy a view and plant your feet on the ground, just as we felt grounded on the water. Slowness meant connectedness. It enhanced human fitness. Fast travel is a mere 100 years old or so — the blink of an eye in human history — and it contributes, I think, to our increasing alienation or disconnect from the Earth and from each other. This contributes to decisions that further alienate us from nature and people.

The past century has seen more destruction to the Earth, to humanity, and to other life forms (hundreds of species extinct) than ever before. I could be wrong, but I believe that travel by car and plane breaks our physical and spiritual links to the Earth, and it is worth remembering that we come from the Earth and ultimately return to it. To my mind, the benefits of modern technology are outweighed by the costs to ourselves, our fellow creatures and our planet. I believe that depression and obesity, among other problems, are linked, at least in part, to our disconnectedness from the Earth and each other. In short, I believe the early Plains Indians had a healthier and more sustainable lifestyle than we do. Their old ways no longer exist because they were overpowered by a more destructive, more numerous and arguably less honourable military force and culture. That victory made our ways dominant, but not necessarily better.

We didn't miss TV at all. Without it, we lived every moment. Life had clearly taken on more zest and enjoyment since we took to the canoe and abandoned TV and the static lifestyle of staying in a house month after month. Travel exposed us to new people, new places and new excitement every day. We hardly ever felt sad. It was great to look forward to each coming day, and to want to get up in the morning. Perhaps it was partly because we had a clear purpose. Everything we did was for getting ourselves to New Orleans. In a word, we were happy.

In this next section, Mark takes a turn at the narrative. He describes Nov. 11, our 72nd day away, by which time we had paddled 2,285 kilometres.

MARK'S ACCOUNT

It's amazing the difference a few days can make. Today as we sped down the Mississippi watching Illinois and Missouri glide silently by, things seemed so perfect. The weather was beautiful with a clear sky and warm sun. All our gear was dry, the scenery was great, a tugboat captain waved at us and we were making excellent time.

My mind wandered back over our trip and I remembered some of the hardships we'd had: fighting wind and waves on the big lakes in Manitoba; the backbreaking drudgery of paddling against the current on the winding Red River; blundering into one of the worst blizzards in the history of the state of Minnesota; the bitter disappointment of having to turn back to Le Sueur after finding the Minnesota River to be frozen; the harrowing experience we had at Lock 13; the disappointment of having to miss a big chunk of the Mississippi River.

All these events seemed so far away today. Far, far away in the distant past, now nothing but open water before us to New Orleans. The Mississippi is such a pleasure to travel. It's beautiful, it's big and best of all, it has a powerful current that helps us immeasurably. I could sit all day and watch the river glide by in its steady, relentless push to the Gulf of Mexico. It fascinates me.

Today we decided to push for distance to see how far we could get. Our original goal was 50 miles (80 kilometres), but we timed ourselves using the mileage markers and found we were doing seven m.p.h., so we knew we could do more than 50. We had to stop early this afternoon as we were out of water and were also in need of bread and a few other supplies. A friendly young man gave me a lift to a grocery store while Brad filled the water containers.

The store was farther away than I thought and I had to walk back, so the whole stop consumed about an hour. However, we had already come 45 miles (72 kilometres) and still had about two hours of daylight left. As the sun began to set and we were approaching the 60-mile mark I turned to Brad and said, "Let's go for 70." He had been thinking the same thing, so we pushed on in the dark, knowing we'd hit 70 around 6 o'clock.

Just after 6, in the twilight, we saw a powerful, sweeping spotlight ahead and numerous other lights. We thought it was a town, but as it approached we suddenly realized the lights were moving toward us. It was a barge and a big one at that! It was quite close to shore, the same shore we were near, so we paddled like mad to land before the wake of the barge hit us. Normally the wake of a barge is no problem for us, but we were awfully close to this one.

All day the banks along the river had been low and smooth, but at this particular point the bank was steep and rocky. We hopped out onto the rocks and held onto the canoe as the waves came crashing in. Several more barges were approaching, so we pulled the canoe and looked for a spot to camp. It was quite an eventful ending to a long day. However, we had paddled 70 miles (113 kilometres), a personal best, and we went to bed with a feeling of accomplishment.

The next morning we awoke to the sound of rain on our tent. The forecast on the radio told us the weather would clear in a little while, so we decided to wait out the rain and let the tent dry. It's nice to have the luxury of time now. Up until this point on our trip we have been constantly driven by time.

We want to make it home for Christmas for various reasons, and we knew we'd have to paddle like madmen to do it. In fact, while we were on the Red River, it looked as if we wouldn't make it. I was a bit worried at the time, as I had a job lined up for the beginning of January, but then I thought, "If the Lord wants us home for Christmas, we'll be home for Christmas." He's looked after us incredibly so far, and He's not going to stop now.

Well, it looks like the Lord wants us home for Christmas. Being forced to miss that chunk of the Mississippi really gives us a lot more time. I jokingly told Brad we can blame my Mom for the snowstorm, as she was praying we'd make it home for Christmas. I was only half joking.

The rain stopped, and the tent was dry by noon, so we were able to get half a day's paddling in. We reached the 60-mile mark (60 miles from Cairo, where a new mile countdown to New Orleans began) and shortly after made camp. It was my turn to set up the tent, while Brad made a delicious stew using the last of the vegetables. Those vegetables had been through so much it's incredible. They'd been frozen and thawed countless times, thrown about, dumped in the bottom of the canoe and stepped on. They were dirty and rubbery, but they sure tasted good!

೨ܐܢ

Mark was not only an excellent paddler; he wrote well, too.

River fog, thick as a blizzard in The Pas, cut our visibility next morning and forced us off the river. Then a commercial fisherman drove up in his skiff. "Where you all from?" he asked, in that classic Southern drawl. We told him. "Tell me this," he continued. "How is it these canoes don't capsize?"

"Ballast," I said. "We're heavy with gear. That weight, riding low, gives us great stability. So when we come to an eddy she may waver a little, but that's all."

We stopped at Cape Girardeau and I visited the editor of the *Southeast Missourian*, a daily newspaper. Hiring was frozen because of the recession. A reporter made only $17,000, he said. But bread was only 29 cents a loaf, a two-pound bag of chips, 69 cents. The cost of living was lower than in Canada.

Courtesy, we constantly find, is the hallmark of U.S. retailers and business people generally. They know how to treat a customer, even a couple of river rats like Mark and I. Waiters and waitresses are also helpful and cheerful. But unlike others who have traveled this river by canoe, we got no free restaurant meals and asked for none. We always offered cash. It's true, though, that rural people gave us a lot of free food.

Back on the river we bucked a headwind for hours and took on some water. Most of the barge captains did their best to help us by gearing down, moving over or waiting until we passed.

BARGES IN OUR DREAMS

Coyotes howled one night, and a strange thing happened to Mark. When one especially loud barge went by as we slept, Mark sat up, shouting, "Look out! Look out! Look out!"

"It's OK, Mark, we're on land, we're safe!"

After a moment he said, "OK," and then lay back, still asleep. Some of our tenser moments surface in our dreams. It's not easy to forget them.

Cairo (pronounced Care-o by locals) has figured in some of Mark Twain's books. The town peaked in the 1950s and then went into decline. When we visited it was hurting. Store after store was for sale or rent. We were told the big companies had pulled out for Florida and other areas. Rural depopulation and stagnation are a problem there as well as in Canada.

The Mississippi there was wider than it was earlier in our trip, and wilder, too. Some days we saw no towns, just river and muddy or rocky banks. In the distance there were beautiful trees, rolling hills, no development — heaven. We knew we were somewhere along the Kentucky (or Tennessee) border. On the radio we found a station from Texas. It was about 15 C most days. That's above zero, T-shirt warm. For mid-November that was sweet, considering temperatures at home in Manitoba would often be below freezing, with snow on the ground.

At night our hands and fingers curled up as if we were still holding a paddle. We could not straighten them, try as we might. And our hands were hard with calluses. We joked that we could grab hot sticks in our fires without a glove. We did that and didn't get burned.

Fog was our new foe. We feared it almost as much as the ice. On Nov. 16 we got off the river at noon after a scary 10-minute dash across open water when we couldn't see anything. What happened is this. We had rounded one of the long "arms" that jut out some 100 metres or so, their purpose being to keep the water high in mid-river for the barges. Instead of following it around to the shore — a long slow process — we headed in at a 45-degree angle, hoping to hit land some distance away to the south, which we finally did.

But in the meantime you're traveling blind, you can't see shore, and you can't see the barges but you hear them. You hear them chugging toward you, and it's frightening, as if they are unstoppable steel monsters out of a science fiction novel. It's a fool's game to travel blind on this river, so we stopped doing so. We were greatly relieved to find shore at last.

As I write at this moment, the groaning engines of a tugboat push a barge slowly past our sandy campsite, somewhere close on the Mississippi. They travel in part by radar, but even they stop in heavy fog. All we see is a blanket of white. At least it's not snow!

CHAPTER 10

SOUTHERN CHARACTERS

A canoe holding a man, his dog and their gear bobbed aimlessly on the river like an errant apple. We first saw them at 8:45 on the morning of Nov. 18, halted on a windy bend with a backdrop of Missouri forest behind them. A big black arrow was painted on the side of the aluminum craft, with "Gulf" in bold letters suggesting their destination.

The black and white dog, a springer spaniel, sat atop a pile of pots and pans, a sleeping cot and boxes and crates of various sizes, all covered partly by an orange tarp. The wind blew hard from the south and caught their canoe and tarp like a sail, stopping them cold, despite the current.

He was a man in his mid-40s, balding, stocky, a PhD and former university fullback. Like thousands of others, Blaine Greer suffered major financial setbacks in the recession of 1990-91. They concerned some rental property. This retired educator (who said he had been a high school principal) had never done much canoeing, but the romance of paddling the length of the Mississippi, which he referred to as the Father of Waters, appealed to him as he sought new meaning at this low ebb in his life.

On Sept. 17 — when we were halfway down Manitoba — he had started at its source, Itasca Lake in Itasca State Park in Minnesota. His first canoe had floated away one night, but that hadn't stopped him. He bought another. With his dog, Shocker ("Got 'im in Wichita!") he was happy. Now he was stymied by wind.

"Don't know what I'll do," he said with a mild drawl, as waves hit and sprayed from the side of his canoe. "Guess I'll head back to New Madrid." Mark and I had stopped at New Madrid for supplies a short distance back. It seemed a shame for him to have to turn around.

"We could tow you!" I said, blurting out an option without even asking my partner. But Mark agreed. "Besides," I added, hoping to make him feel better, "we could use the company." We tied a rope to our stern and his bow and pulled him for the rest of that day and well into the next. He paddled too, of course, and it was one of our most difficult days on the river, not because of our friend but because of the relentless wind.

At almost every turn on the winding Mississippi we encountered wind and waves. Like the Red, the Mississippi meanders freely, doubling back on itself and twisting like a snake. Waves frequently washed over our splash cover and a lot of water sloshed into the bottom of Jimmy-Jock. Blaine and Shocker took on a lot of water too. I know they bailed now and then. It rained steadily. We would paddle for an hour or so and then pause to scoop out about 10 ice-cream pails of water. It was exciting, even in the rain, and far better than being in the tent, an option we dismissed.

Our mission was important, for Blaine had an appointment to keep with his wife. He had to be in Carruthersville to meet her next day at noon. She was driving in, if I recall, from their home in Cape Girardeau, two hours north. We arrived in Carruthersville on time and had a delicious catfish supper with her and Blaine, who picked up the tab.

"Well, I'm grateful to you guys for towing me all day yesterday. I'd still be back there if you hadn't." Blaine also gave us his U.S. Army Corps of Engineers maps of the Mississippi. They made it possible to safely navigate the river by knowing where the barges would be in relation to the green and red buoys. Those maps also point out obstacles, dikes, towns and the like. (We really had no business being on the water without them. We sometimes got in the way of barges because we didn't know how the buoy system worked, or where the river was going.) We were grateful to get the maps and happy we'd been of help.

TORNADO WARNING

It was just as well we had to stop at noon for the catfish lunch, because a tornado warning was issued. A man named Larry, a Vietnam vet who managed and owned Ezra's Landing Restaurant, advised us to heed it and stay off the water. Well, the last time we ignored advice to wait we had to be rescued by a tugboat from an ice jam. So we waited, not wanting to tangle with a tornado.

As we moved our gear up from shore near an out building near Ezra's Landing, a fellow of about 60 approached us. "Y'all figurin' to leave yer gear there?" he asked.

"Sure," I said, "it should be OK."

"I wouldn't," he replied. "There's black folks aroun' might git at it."

I paused a moment or two and looked at him again. "You know, sir," I said with a smile, "it sounds to me like you are a little bit prejudiced."

Then came his classic rejoinder. I shall never forget this as long as I live: "I'm not prejudiced," he announced. "I jus' don't like niggers!"

We were, indeed, entering the great American South. Carruthersville is a typical Missouri town of 7,500, near the border of Arkansas. The eastern shore was part of beautiful Tennessee. We were entering one of the wilder and greener stretches of the river and one of the poorer regions of the United States, where unemployment was high and towns were struggling. For many, the old stereotypes persisted.

Mark had a brainstorm next day while we waited out the tornado threat and did laundry. "Maybe we could leave our heavy winter gear with Larry and pick it up on the way home." It weighed a lot and took up space — snowmobile suits, boots, mitts, you name it. We left it behind thanks to Larry's help. He also treated us to another great southern meal — barbecued pork and beans, fries, black-eyed pea soup, for only $5. (Sadly, Mark tells me that Ezra's Landing was washed away by the terrible flooding that struck the Mississippi in the mid-1990s. But I believe Larry was not hurt.)

Back on the water next day, the worst of the storm having passed us by, we were lighter! And floating higher! Which we really liked. We looked like we did when we left The Pas Sept. 1. The distance from water to top of gunnel is called freeboard; more is better in rough water. Mark had already given one of his sleeping bags to Blaine, who had none.

The night we camped with Blaine was interesting, as it contrasted our different habits. We used a canvas tent, air mattresses and sleeping bags, and put the tent high and dry on a grassy bank. Blaine preferred to sleep on his cot by the water's edge in the open air. He wrapped the tarp around himself and hoped for the best. Next morning he looked groggy. He announced that he'd had a rough night. The wind had got up and torn the tarp away, and he'd gone running down the shore to catch it. It had also rained. Blaine was a wet and unhappy camper when we emerged warm and dry from our beds.

I admired his habits of personal hygiene, however. We watched as he washed his head and face thoroughly when our paddling day ended. "It's important to keep your head clean," he told us. "It keeps you feeling well." I've since made that a practice on canoe trips and I endorse it, just as I do the importance of warm, clean feet. It seems if you can keep your top and bottom parts happy, the rest of the body, and the all-important mind, are also better off.

One of Blaine's practices that we didn't try was the drinking of a little Mississippi water. It didn't seem to hurt him, but we took a pass. Years later, during our second trip on the Mississippi, I did drink a little water with no apparent ill effect.

We and Blaine went our separate ways after that, but I was to meet up with him again four years later in Manitoba's north.

We met another fellow, named Bob, on the river north of Carruthersville, just prior to our meeting Blaine. Bob was also in his 40s (what is it about man's fifth decade that prompts such freedom-loving behaviour?). He had built himself a rowboat, but not just any old rowboat. This one was big — seven metres long, with a closed cabin for sleeping and cooking. Bob had left West Virginia in March, and he was simply floating out near the middle of the river when we met him, idly dipping his oars from time to time.

"I'm safe here," he said, as a big barge chugged toward us. "They stay between the green buoys and the red ones (along the far shore)."

"We didn't know that, Bob. Thanks."

"Where's your map?" We'd been using highway maps or my atlas, when we bothered using any at all. Usually we just went with the river and took what we got. "Well, good luck," he said, probably thinking those Canadian fools are going to need it. That's why we were so glad to receive Blaine's gift of his maps. Blaine might well have saved us; the maps are that important. Even with them, we had some close calls ahead.

Another man near New Madrid just happened to be in his boat when we passed by. This teacher of environmental ecology warned us about the three-metre drop from a control dam on the river ahead, and showed us the way around an island to avoid it. This is the kind of good fortune that constantly shone upon us. Maybe a guardian angel or two were involved.

Nov. 21 was Day 82 of our trip and mile 1,681 (kilometre 2,705) paddled. I crawled from the tent and heard a tractor approaching. It was 6:30 a.m. and dawn was just breaking. We were high on a bank above the river on the Arkansas side. "We've got a visitor," I told Mark, who was packing up inside.

I watched as an old tractor driven by an even older man came into view. The tractor towed an aluminum fishing boat on a trailer along a grassy path to the river. I waved and smiled, and he climbed off his old machine and approached.

ROBERT E. LEE

"Sorry if we're on your land," I said. "We'll be gone in a few minutes."

"No need to worry," he said. "What are you-all doing?"

As Mark crawled from the tent I introduced us and said we were from Canada and headed for New Orleans. "And what's your name?"

The old man smiled. It took him a bit to get the words out, for without realizing it I had set up one of his favourite moments. "Ma name's Robert E. Lee," he announced with his drawl, the grin now broad across his deeply lined face.

"Robert E. Lee!" I said, with appropriate respect. "I may be a Canadian, but I know the Civil War. Are you related to *the* Robert E. Lee, that great Confederate general?"

The grin remained as he said, "Weeellllll — no. A lot of people have a double take when I tell them, though."

"I'll bet they do," I said. "So where do you live?"

"Tomato, Arkansas."

"Tomato? Many folks live there?"

"No, but we've still got a post office. We're proud o'that," said Mr. Lee. We learned that he was a 74-year-old farmer and commercial fisherman. "You're goin' to N'Orleans? A've neva been there."

"Never been to New Orleans?" I said, surprised. Then he mentioned some places a few hundred kilometres north and south — the limits of his lifelong travels. Our talk turned to the river, his fishing, his home.

"I've met so many nice people come down this river, and some real oddball outfits too. One time I was with my grandson and he saw something up the river. 'What is it?' I asked him.

"'Gramps, you ain't gonna believe this,' he said.

"'Well, try me,' I said.

"'It's a school bus.'

"'A school bus! Nooo!'

"'Yes,' he said.

A retired couple had sold their Wisconsin house, bought the bus, put it on floats, powered it with an outboard, customized the interior and made it their home. The last he heard they were down in the Gulf of Mexico, south of New Orleans. They sent him a Christmas card every year.

Robert E. Lee told us another story. He once watched a large raft float by — with 20 college girls and one 60-year-old "maintenance man." The girls asked him along so he went.

"And those girls," Robert said, "they had such nice tans."

Robert had to pull in his nets and we had to paddle, so we said our goodbyes and began our day in earnest.

At day's end we sat around our little fire chatting, writing and admiring the sepia beauty of the descending night. Then a strange thing happened. A voice called out from the river: "Are you OK? Are you stranded?"

"We're fine," Mark shouted in reply. We then invited the man to join us for a bite of our stew. What a fine big fellow he was! Bob, 34, was a true man of the river, a trapper, fisherman, hunter — a big strapping southerner. He was tall, broad-shouldered and good-natured and we welcomed him to our fire.

As he strode toward us from his boat, a dandy big knife hung at his side. "Wow, that's a beaut!" I said, and he handed it to me to inspect. I unsheathed mine — a U.S. navy-issue Seabee that Dad had found in the U.S.

"Wow, am I safe?" he said in mock concern, and seemed pleased that I admired American workmanship. He had been hunting deer, with no success. But success for a man like him is just being there, enjoying this little wilderness, his home.

He said he envied us, once he heard how far we'd come. We've been told that by other young men: "You're doing what I've dreamed of doing but never had the courage to do."

MEMPHIS, AND ELVIS

A feeling of joy gripped us next day as we watched the skyline of Memphis, jagged with skyscrapers, loom before us. The place where Elvis Presley got his start. This was our last big city before New Orleans, and we got to it mid-morning, docking at a marina in Memphis Harbour, our Canadian flag flapping behind us.

But Memphis was not a joy. We had wanted to eat at a Bonanza buffet, but it was too far away. That meant leaving the canoe alone for too long. We forgot to mail postcards. These reasons may sound lame, but they disappointed us. Nor did we hear any live blues on Beale Street, as we left early. In hindsight, we probably should have spent one night in Memphis, but we couldn't find a decent campsite.

We didn't even laugh there. We met a panhandler, a tall thin man who moved on when we gave nothing. "Just a few spare pennies?" he pleaded. I probably should have helped him out, but he came on so strongly that we put up a barrier. I felt bad about not giving him money.

Then came a hustler. We had him pegged from the start.

"Hey, you lookin' for work?"

Mark and I were eating a pound cake on the grass in a park near the river when the young black man approached us.

"Hey, you guys know a guy named Bob?" We did, the rowboat man, but denied it.

"You lookin' for work? The barges are hiring," he continued. "They always need hands. Ten dollars an hour, 30 days on, 30 off. It's dangerous work, but the money's good. They pay a 16-hour day, and for most of that you can read in your bunk. I'm a cook, and I make $15 an hour."

"Interesting. But we don't need work right now, thanks." I brought out my knife and cut our cake with it, handing another piece to Mark. He offered it to the man, who declined.

I cut more cake and laid down the knife in view, close at hand. I was ready, expecting the worst. More small talk followed. These hustlers are all the same, I thought, whether in North America or North Africa. He finally got around to his true purpose, which would be either an attempt to rob us if he had a gun, or a pitch to sell us drugs. I suspected the latter, since this was midday and there were two of us.

"You guys want to buy a toke?" The question came out of the blue, unconnected to his other idle chatter.

"We don't smoke, thanks." And as abruptly as he came, he left.

We left Memphis disappointed. We tend not to click well with cities, preferring the friendlier people of towns and the shorter walking distances. There was no good place to camp for the night. The closest we got to the blues was a statue of Elvis Presley on Beale Street. Oh well. We had our bad days too.

Next day, Day 83 of the trip and mile 1,755 (kilometer 2,856) we bucked a strong northwest wind but still did 45 miles 72 kilometres. We typically ate lunch in the canoe, one of us paddling while the other made sandwiches, handing them over on the blade of his paddle. A cold front was due in that night, so we paddled as far south as we could.

But we hit rapids. "Keep her floating no matter what!" I said as we hit yet another rough spot. The splash cover kept out most of the water. Mark had superb balance and nerves of steel. Being in the cockpit of the splash cover, he had the most to lose if we tipped, for it might not be quick and easy for him to get free. Yet he never said boo.

We enjoyed the rough spots. They were exciting. They tested us. But we did take precautions. At one point the river narrowed and the current increased sharply, what's called the venturi effect. At that point we met an oncoming barge, and rather than risk being swept beneath it, I chose the safer path by landing. My object was to get us home in a car, not a coffin, and so far we'd done pretty well.

CHAPTER 11

ALLIGATORS AND WHIRLPOOLS

Mark Bergen continues the narrative.

"Alligator stabbers!" Brad's voice rang through the little grocery/hardware store, and I looked around to see if anyone heard him. He was showing me a butcher knife — a large butcher knife. In fact, it looked more like a machete. "This sucker will puncture their skins no problem," he laughed.

We had been warned about alligators by Blaine, the canoeist we had met who was paddling the Mississippi with his springer spaniel, Shocker. At first we thought he was joking, but he was dead serious. "There are plenty of alligators in Louisiana," he told us. "I don't mean to scare you, but these animals are killing machines. They prey at night on anything near the water."

Blaine went on to tell us that although alligators had been an endangered species years ago because of skin hunters, they were making a real comeback because of protective laws. In fact, they were quite numerous.

His words rang in my mind as Brad laughingly showed me the knife. We were in a little town in Mississippi called Friar's Point. It was an interesting, unmistakably southern town with a few buildings, a small gas station with a couple of ancient gas pumps out front, and a few men standing by them, watching us. "Whew-wee! We got us a couple o' *honkies!*" one fellow exclaimed as we walked past. (We waved and smiled back.) The little store we found sold everything from TVs to corn flakes and it was here that Brad found the Alligator Stabber.

He bought two of them and joked about it as we trudged back through some woods to the canoe. Suddenly a compact truck lurched up beside us and a portly, bearded man peered out at us. He was a deer hunter. And we were on his hunting club's land.

He was quite an amiable fellow once we explained our situation, and we asked him about alligators along the Mississippi River. He didn't know a lot, but he did know that alligators had been reported to be just a short distance down the river. However, he had never heard of anyone being killed by one — a reassuring statement to be sure.

Alligators aside, though, we had a great day. We had great weather, saw an interesting town, made good distance, and found an ideal campsite. A very unusual day for us in that everything seemed to go just right.

The Mississippi River never ceases to amaze me. Not just its size, power and grandeur, but also the fact that it is a wilderness river. I expected its banks to be heavily populated with lots of cottages, houses and small towns as well as big cities. I thought we'd have a tough time finding campsites with any privacy.

Nothing could be further from the truth. We can paddle for hours and not see a single soul. The towns are few and far between and there are almost no houses on the river. True, there are always barges going up and down, but even they have few signs of humanity. All we see is a tugboat pushing any number of barges, and we rarely see the people working on them.

Instead we see trees, bushes, sandbars and wildlife. We rarely have to worry about getting a secluded campsite. The whole river is secluded. We often hear coyotes howling and yipping at night. Besides the barges (and we only see one or two an hour), the stillness is broken only by the lapping of the waves on shore, the honk of Canada geese and our own paddles dipping in the muddy water.

I love the seclusion, the ruggedness, the freedom of the Mississippi River. Brad and I both feel more at home on the river than we do in the cities. Life on the Mississippi is going to be a hard habit to break. I'm glad I have a place like The Pas to come home to and not a mass of steel, concrete and glass like Memphis, St. Louis or Winnipeg.

Brad resumes the narrative.

I've still got my alligator stabber — in its original case!

On Nov. 27 and for the third day in a row, we did 50 miles

(80 kilometres) or better. To do that we rose at 5:30 and were on the water an hour later. This day we didn't start paddling until 7:15, but we took a shortcut that saved us at least 20 minutes. But for a minute or two Walter Koshel's warnings about shortcuts being hazardous came to mind. You'll recall the trip near The Pas that he and I did together.

"Feel like taking a shortcut?" I asked Mark, as we glided down the river. "We could cut this corner. The map shows one dike, then a clear channel."

"Sure," Mark replied, after a moment's thought. "Let's go for it."

A dike could be one of two things. It could be a long narrow pile of *visible* rocks that jutted a couple of hundred metres into the river to keep the centre deep for barges, which is what I thought we'd find. Or it could be an *underwater* pile of rocks that kept the water up, but which, more importantly to us, tended to create rapids and/or whirlpools. The latter is what we found.

From afar, it looked innocent enough. We hit the turbulent water — and then got quite a surprise. To our right, yawning wide like a giant's mouth, was a whirlpool. Shaped like a funnel, it narrowed into the depths.

"Look at that!" shouted Mark. We pried hard to get on the edge of it rather than hit it square on and risk the bow going down. We caught that edge and for a moment that seemed much longer, I peered down into a deep swirling hole. I would have found it hard to believe had I not seen it with my own eyes. It was as if we were in a gigantic bathtub and riding the edge as the water swirled down the drain.

Fortunately, we didn't go down with it. Being heavy has its benefits. But our respect for the river was ratcheted up another notch.

ာ◆ာ

Southern hospitality is something of a legend across North America, and Mark and I can vouch for it. It was Nov. 28, America's Thanksgiving Day, and we weren't aware of that. We stopped at Mayersville, Miss., population 400, as we needed some peanut butter and water. We hiked over the levee that separated every community down there from the great river, protecting them from spring flooding, and entered the little town. The one store we found had no peanut butter, so we continued to walk down the street in hopes of finding another.

THANKSGIVING DAY

Most of the homes were humble dwellings, some of them dilapidated. In contrast, a big white house on a corner stood out from all the rest. It had a verandah, like the old house my grandfather, Dr. Bird, had in Boissevain. In fact it looked a lot like the house he kept — fresh paint, lawn furniture, beautiful trees in the yard. Six people, three men and two girls and a woman, sat and chatted as we approached. It looked like a scene from *Gone with the Wind*.

"What do you think?" I asked Mark.

"Let's go for it," he said.

"Hello!" I said to the family, as we stopped at the edge of their driveway.

"Hello," a woman replied.

I explained our situation and asked if we could buy some peanut butter.

They all stopped and stared. After a moment's pause the older woman who had said hello responded and sent a girl into the house. Presently the girl returned with a two-pound jar. She gave it to a man who brought it to us. He refused our money.

"Listen, thank you very much," I said sincerely. "This will ensure that we have a good supper." And we turned to go.

"Wait!" said the woman. We stopped. Had we done something or said something wrong? "Please come and join us," she continued. "It's Thanksgiving. We just finished eating, but there's lots left."

"Are you sure?" I said. Mark and I were dirty, unshaven, sunburned and hungry.

"Yes. Y'all come on up on the verandah."

Mark looked at me and I looked at him and — well, we soon thought we'd died and gone to heaven! Plates piled high with turkey, dressing, corn and sweet potatoes were set before us by the girls. We hadn't eaten such a meal since we'd left his aunt's place in Winnipeg. Home-cooked and scrumptious. Big second helpings, then dessert: a plate for each of us with *three* pieces of pie — sweet potato, lemon and pecan, with the pecan made from nuts off their own tree!

As we ate, they plied us with questions. Where had we come from? What had we seen? Why were we doing it? How long had we been away? Where were we going? We asked a few questions ourselves and learned this was the home of Herbert Herman, Mayerville's postmaster. The children brought out a road atlas and we showed them how far we had come, and what our route had been. They were impressed.

The isolated and wild north shore of Lake Winnipeg offers miles of sandy beaches, shallow surf and beautiful wild flowers.

In the vicinity of Robinson Lake, northeast of Norway House, I came across the men above. That's Hubert Folster standing at the rear. He gave me a pike, but I already had two of my own.

Action Packers kept the load low and tidy; the barrel held my camera and other valuables. An important benefit: they didn't catch the wind.

A fishing guide on Elbow Lake, north of Oxford House, hoists a nice pike for this European family.

Here is Jimmy-Jock in a rare moment of peace during my journey from The Pas to York Factory in the summer of 1995. Behind it is the Hayes River, which rushes toward the Arctic with particular fury for about 38 kilometres. It's a beautiful country, with excellent fishing.

On Aug. 12, 1995, I arrived at York Factory with my new friends from Winnipeg.

My new friends and I paddle toward Hudson's Bay and an overcast sky that had dumped a lot of rain on the region. It was cold, too, and fortunately we encountered no polar bears.

This is Blaine Greer, a man who was pursuing his own voyage of discovery when we became friends.

We tow Blaine Greer, near Carruthersville, Mo.

'Bob' in his rowboat on the Mississippi. He was from West Virginia.

The Halloween blizzard of 1991 hit Minnesota hard, leaving more than 20 inches of snow in its wake after two days. We camped and paddled in the middle of it before the frozen river forced us to make a hard decision.

Fog and barges made life interesting on the Mississippi. This was near Carruthersville, Mo., in 1991.

We entered the Mississippi River for the first time, at Dubuque, Iowa.

We were paddling closer to New Orleans.

Robert E. Lee,
of Tomato, Arkansas.

Shaving was done for special occasions, such as a restaurant
meal or visit to a church.

Mark on the Mississippi.

Mark and I shake hands after reaching St. Louis after three weeks. For me it was a major milestone, as it meant the completion of a journey across the length of North America. It meant a lot to Mark, too.

It was a lovely hour we shared with Mr. Herman and his family and we'll always be grateful for such wonderful hospitality and sharing. It was great to sit back, relax and watch children play in their yard. They said we'd made their day too, which made us feel good.

We bid them a warm farewell and headed back to Jimmy-Jock, who, like us, was always eager to get going. On the way to the canoe we saw our first cotton field, with little white tufts of the stuff clinging to the plants. We saw that some people grew cactus as an attractive shrub-like lawn ornament. In chatting with a lady we learned that most of the work was seasonal — harvesting cotton and soybeans, which helped to explain the run-down appearance of the place. "We need industry," the social worker told us. In that sense Mayersville was much like many small communities across Western Canada.

Back on the river, we were forced by two barges to go ashore in a narrow channel, and Mark suggested we camp right there, early. It was 3:50. As he raised the tent and I started a fire, two men approached. They arrived in a pickup truck along the nearby country road, which we hadn't seen.

"Hope we're not trespassing," I said, always hoping to head off a conflict before one began.

"No problem," replied big Bob Wallis. He introduced the younger man as his son-in-law. "You've got a federal law giving you a right to 50 feet of this shore. Where are you from?"

After we explained, they insisted we accept a bagful of locally grown tangerines, a hatchet, toilet paper (we needed this more than the other stuff!), a gallon of unopened spring water and duct tape. Incredible generosity. And he topped that off with good information about the river and New Orleans.

Thanksgiving Day. We had a great deal to be thankful for. This was living, connecting with people and sharing our story. At the same time, we were missing our homes in The Pas. We'd been away a long time and looked forward with great anticipation to being home before Christmas.

On Nov. 29 we reached a milestone, our 2,000th mile paddled (3,320 kilometres). We were just north of Vicksburg, Miss., a famous Confederate stronghold during the Civil War. It fell to the Union armies on July 4, 1863, after a long siege.

HISTORIC VICKSBURG

We spent much of the next day visiting Vicksburg, which had about 40,000 people. We would have quickly left after buying supplies, had I not phoned home. Dad encouraged us to slow down and take in the sights of this historic city, and we're glad we did. The old courthouse museum held us spellbound for hours. Built in 1858 by slave labour, the building survived a 47-day siege with only one serious hit. It was filled with early Americana and items from the war: swords, pistols, a Confederate flag, even displays about early newspaper people. One of them, J. M. Sands, published the *Vicksburg Daily Citizen*.

During the siege, Mr. Sands ran out of newsprint but that didn't silence him. He stripped the walls and used wallpaper. He strongly backed the Southern cause, as in this example:

> "We lay before our readers in this issue an account of [General Robert E.] Lee's brilliant and successful onslaught upon the abolition hordes and show ... how our gallant boys of the cavalry have fleshed their swords to the hilt with their vaunting foe, and how each musket of the infantry had told its fatal leaden tale....
> Success and glory to our arms! God and right are with us."

Interestingly, abolitionists such as Harriet Beecher Stowe also claimed God's support and the moral high ground. Her novel *Uncle Tom's Cabin* did much to end slavery.

Then there was Mary Dawson Cairn, who published and edited a weekly newspaper in Mississippi from 1937 to 1980 or so. She stood for self-reliance, low taxes, small government and unfettered freedom of the press. The museum curator I spoke to had worked for her as a reporter, and he called her a marvelous woman. At one point in the 1950s she refused to pay a $47 tax, a new government levy. After the Internal Revenue Service padlocked her paper's door in an effort to shut it down, Cairn left her sick bed to cut the lock with a hacksaw, and proceeded to put out that week's edition!

Leaving the museum, we bought groceries and headed back to Jimmy-Jock, whom we had hidden in the tangled growth along shore. It poured rain as we tucked into a gallon of ice cream and cake. "Good thing we didn't stop for lunch," Mark joked, "otherwise we wouldn't have had room for what was really important."

"A touch damp, is it not?" I said, as we huddled over our ice cream and cake in the pouring rain.

"Just a bit," he replied, as water streamed off his leather cowboy hat.

Mississippi fog blanketed the river as we hugged the east shore. We heard a barge coming and made sure we were close to the bank. By 4:30 we found a nice campsite and cooked our chicken legs — seven for $1.90. Roasted golden brown, they tasted good. We never did see any alligators, but with our "stabbers" we were ready.

CHAPTER 12

NEW ORLEANS!

D ec. 1, 1991. We were on the home stretch. It rained, and it was Sunday, so we rested and read. We took turns reading the Bible, a practice we followed pretty well from the start. This week it was chapters in Ephesians. In a way this was fitting, as Ephesians is said to have been written by the Apostle Paul who, like us, traveled great distances, though for a different purpose.

We put plastic garbage bags on the tent this day, as we were getting wet. The old tent needed waterproofing after all the use and abuse. We were only 482 kilometres north of New Orleans. But it kept raining and blowing, right through the night.

Next day at 10:30 a.m., during a pause in the downpour, we resolved to pack up and paddle. Mark was eager to go. He couldn't very well go for a walk — deer season was on, and he could have got shot — so we decided to leave.

As luck would have it, no sooner did we pack up than a big bank of fog rolled in. Fog and rain had dogged us for weeks. The wind picked up and it got colder. Through the rain and fog we paddled on, bowing our heads and making pretty good time.

Torrential rain came next, combined with the prospect of falling temperatures (it was supposed to fall to near freezing that night). So we decided to camp at 2 p.m. This time we put the splash cover underneath and the bags and fly on top, and then scurried in.

Gee, it was nice to be dry! Dryness for us was only one step short of warmth. Often, those days, we were damp and chilled. There was no way around it, living as we did. My Gore-Tex jacket kept my top dry, but my legs were exposed in my slacks, as were Mark's.

We had learned to be thankful for little blessings: dryness, warmth, sunshine. We found we didn't need other things: TV, cars, boots, tables, chairs, stereos, etc. Even the journal that forms the basis of this book was handwritten with a Bic pen on looseleaf paper.

We looked forward to the end. We'd been away a long time. After some days of leisure in New Orleans we'd drive home. Then we would have to fit all the usual stuff back into our lives. It would fit, because it fit that other lifestyle. Frankly, I looked forward to sleeping in my big bed again, with Athena at my feet.

Dec. 2, windy and rainy, was Mark's 20th birthday. We celebrated.

We arrived next day at Natchez, 426 kilometres from New Orleans, camped nearby and walked into the old city, finding a restaurant called The Grill that specialized in catfish. We had talked about having a nice catfish meal, and for $9.95 we got one, with grilled catfish, stuffed baked potato, kaiser bun and salad. We agreed, though, that however nice it was, our stews were better.

For example, there was Mississippi Surprise, Mark's creation. Ingredients: One bird's nest, a cup of elbow macaroni, oriental noodles, three potatoes, two carrots, (chopped), some ketchup, tin of tuna, grated cheddar and a half cup rice. Method: start fire with bird's nest. Add wood to create medium-high heat. Fill coffee can one-third full of water and the rest of the ingredients. Simmer 10 to 15 minutes, or until you can't wait any longer. Add raisins if you like, and more water if it becomes too sticky. Top it off with a cinnamon bun roasted on a stick.

It's called surprise because Mark surprised me by throwing all we had into it. Usually we had two kinds of stews, one mainly macaroni, the other mainly vegetables. He combined the two.

An absolutely beautiful day, 18 C and sunny. Almost no wind and not a cloud in the sky. All day we saw only four barges. We saw our first paddlewheel boat, the Mississippi Queen, a grand old vessel with five decks. It was a floating casino and restaurant, and it looked beautiful, white and red and black, against the green backdrop of the rolling hills. Even our campsite was especially pretty, with a good view of the river.

AN ALLIGATOR TRAPPER

An old Ford truck splattered with mud pulled up beside us as we trudged along a levee near Morganza, Miss. where we had stopped for supplies. Each levee, or ridge, had a road on top. "Care for a ride?" said the young man, whose name was Vic. "I'll take you back to your boat."

"Sounds good," I said, and Mark and I hopped into the truck's cluttered box. Back at the canoe, Vic had news. "River's going to rise 10 feet. You'd best not be on it when it does."

"By when, Vic?" I asked, as Mark put away our groceries.

In three or four days, he said. All the rain that had hit the central U.S. would fill the Ohio River which flows into the Mississippi at Cairo 1,200 kilometres north of where we were. The rain fills the sloughs and ponds. Then it raises the river, with nowhere else to go.

"By then we should be in New Orleans, Vic."

"Good, because this river is rough. It killed my brother. He drowned just a few miles from here. The river sucked him and his whole bathtub [flat-bottomed skiff] right under. I'd hate for that to happen to you. Your little boat would be sucked under too."

Vic then explained eddies that created whirlpools. Another man had told us he'd seen one suck down a whole tree and then spit it out like a missile.

"Are there any alligators around here?" Mark asked.

"Sure. In fact I trapped the state record," Vic said proudly. "A 14-foot, 752-pounder."

"Wow!" we exclaimed. "Near here?"

"Two miles from here."

"How do you trap them?"

"We use a big hook, and a chicken for bait. When we haul the gator up and get its head above water, we shoot it where its ear would be. That does it."

"When is the season?"

"September. And I got $68 per foot for that alligator."

"Where do you sell it?" Mark asked.

"Right here in town. Buyers come, and we sell to the highest bidder."

"Interesting," I said. "Any around here now?"

"Not likely," Vic said. He explained that the reptiles, which can run faster than a man, move away from the river into ponds in December. There they mate.

"So how does one fend off an alligator?"

"Climb a tree!" Vic said. "They're fast. But they won't likely attack unless they're with young."

Next day, Dec. 6, we paddled 100 kilometres. "How ya doin', Canada!" someone shouted from shore, noticing our big Canadian flag. It drew a lot of attention. Men in small boats often stopped to talk, offering advice and encouragement.

"Do you need anything? Would you like some coffee?" shouted a man from a tug in the Baton Rouge harbour. We declined but thanked him, preferring to make time paddling.

From Baton Rouge south, the river was deep enough for ocean-going vessels. One ship looked like a gigantic sausage. It hardly made any wake as it passed us by. These ships were huge, and we felt so tiny in our canoe.

Dec. 7 was the 50th anniversary of Japan's attack on Pearl Harbour and here it was a day of remembrance, a day to honour those who died in that event that drew the United States into the Second World War. This ultimately sealed victory for the Allies and freedom for us in North America. Without that victory, we likely would not have been free to make this canoe trip.

In Donaldsonville, where we stopped for water, we saw some TV coverage of it in a restaurant. We also saw the town's Santa Claus parade.

CANCER ALLEY

Cancer Alley stretches along the Mississippi River between New Orleans and the industrial city of Baton Rouge, 217 kilometres away. The river was no longer the wilderness we had come to enjoy but an endless chain of chemical plants. They spewed tonnes of particles into the air, blanketing the region in an almost constant haze that was linked to illnesses, hence the name.

We sneezed, and our throats had more than the usual phlegm. Our eyes were sore and irritated. "I wouldn't live here," the first mate on a barge told us. Yet many do, for the jobs. We wanted out fast. We couldn't even find a peaceful campsite. Factories hummed and clanged all night, and you can imagine the increase in barge traffic. We slept fitfully.

On Sunday Dec. 8, Day 99 of the trip, we paddled half a day and did 47 kilometres. There was at least one barge at every turn. Large dock-like structures extended far into the river from the chemical plants, adding to the hazards. To steer around these was to expose ourselves to the central channel where the fast and gigantic ocean-goers were.

Heading south, the channel was marked by green floating buoys on the right and red ones on the left. The ships had to stay between them or risk running aground. That meant we needed to keep to the right of the green buoys or to the left of the red ones, to be safest. The green buoys were rectangular, the red ones conical, and they were anchored. They rocked back and forth in the current. We'd come close to hitting one or two, which would not have been pretty, as each was almost as big as a fridge.

We found it was not a good practice to stay on one side of the channel. One reason was that the best current was near the middle, so often we went there. Another reason was that the outside of a curve is bad news. Not only is it the long way around a bend, it's also where the worst waves end up from passing barges. Some of those waves could have sunk us.

And so we crossed the river back and forth from time to time. This too was risky, and we took great care, as the river was five kilometers wide in places. We typically looked down the river 16 kilometres to the next bend, and were good judges of distance since we'd been doing it for three months.

This was our last night on the river. Hard to believe. That seemed sad. I really didn't want it to end. I didn't feel accomplishment as much as let down. It was a time of mixed feelings, because part of us longed for home. We found a pretty good place to camp without too many burrs. The burrs down there were super-sharp and plentiful. We pulled up some of the tall plants or hacked them down with our paddles. I'm sure the burrs in a pasture up in Minnesota had punctured the polypropylene bottom of my tent.

LAST SUPPER

The last supper. It was Mark's turn to cook and he did a splendid job as usual. For some time now we'd been cooking up extra stew and eating it cold at breakfast. As we sat around a fire with our stew we heard an animal rustling in the leaves behind us. Mark shone his light into the willows and we saw our first possum. It was half the size of an adult raccoon and could it ever run.

As our fire burned down this warm evening, both of us lost in our thoughts, I went over the trip in my mind. We'd met a dog that tried to eat my cat, had been arrested at the U.S. border, been caught smack dab in the middle of a blizzard in Minnesota, frozen by record-low temperatures that fell to -12 C, soaked to the skin by torrential rains, stuck in pack ice on the Mississippi and rescued by a tugboat. We'd been hungry and almost out of food, thirsty and almost out of water. We'd run rapids and struck boulders. We'd ridden the edge of a whirlpool and stared into its depths. The canoe had been broken in six places by ice and rock. We rode the rollers of lakes Manitoba, Winnipegosis and Cedar, when people thought we were crazy. Well, folks, we've almost made it. Not once did we capsize. And through it all, we met many wonderful people.

৩৽৶

December 9, 1991, Day 100, Mile 2,353, Kilometre 3787

This was it — D-Day. Destination Day. Every body of water had challenged us right to the end, and the Mississippi was no exception. We got on the river before sunup. At 6:20, stars still twinkled through the morning haze. Fog rolled in and forced us to hug the shore.

Trouble was, this was a busy shoreline. Many barges were parked. Tugboats sorted them and moved them the same way that rail cars were shunted back and forth at The Pas.

They were a menace, and at one point I had a particularly strong sense of danger. The fog was so thick that we couldn't see more than 40 metres ahead. I cut over from the channel and stopped us cold alongside a parked barge, and that was a good thing. Seconds later a barge came toward us along the same route we had been on. It might have hit us.

While Mark rested and read, I climbed a ladder on the barge to get a better view of the river. Up higher, I could see we needed to skirt around two large barges. A tug came close and a man asked if we needed help around the big tubs. I declined, though I should have accepted. We moved on.

More fog rolled in, making matters worse. Again I steered quickly toward a parked barge. We were only 47 kilometres from New Orleans and if we weren't really careful we wouldn't get there. After coming this far, through so much, that would be doubly tragic.

When in doubt, do nothing. We hung on and waited. Then a voice came over a megaphone from the tugboat 50 metres in front of us. "You in the canoe, can you hear me? You're welcome to come aboard my tug. Paddle alongside and tie up there."

We did, and what a great visit it turned out to be. That was the one thing Mark and I had talked about but hadn't yet done — seen the inside of a tugboat. This one was called the Captain Briscoe, and we boarded it with the help of deckhand Jim Hayes. Jim was bearded and in his 20s, and had only been working there a few months.

He showed us into the dining area, a small room off the kitchen, where we met Second Mate David Severs. David was taken with our trip and mentioned an interest in doing it himself, one day. It was just 7:30 a.m. and they had already eaten. We tucked into leftover biscuits, gravy and sausages. Then Jim gave us a tour. We saw the small cabin for visitors, and also the engine room and the den-like living room.

Soon the captain himself, 51-year-old Robert Byrd, gave us a tour of his pilot's cabin, which sat high above the rest of the boat. Mr. Byrd told us the Captain Briscoe was named after its owner. It was 155 feet (47 metres) long and 50 feet (15 metres) wide, with 5,600 h.p. generated by two 16-cylinder GM engines. He was waiting for orders to push nine barges upstream. Each 300-foot (91-metre) barge carried 3,000 tonnes of cargo. Empty, the barges, which resemble bathtubs, weighed 2,000 tonnes.

It felt great to see the inside of a captain's cabin after weeks of watching them from afar. Windows filled three sides of the cabin, giving him excellent visibility. You could see everything for miles around. Inside was a big round radar screen. Byrd said canoes appeared to be logs on the screen, and tugs ran over logs. Sometimes a canoe's movement tipped a captain off to its true identity.

After a three-hour visit we said our goodbyes and returned to the water, where we paddled with renewed vigour, feeling better. We saw ships from South America, Europe and Asia. Sometimes we even saw their crewmen, and wondered how they felt so far from home.

Closer to the city we saw the shipyards where the big vessels were maintained and repaired. A brutal east wind gave us trouble near the end. We took on some water and had to paddle hard through whitecaps.

SHOUTS OF CONGRATULATIONS

A series of wharfs lined both sides of the river. Men who worked on them often came to watch us pass, shouting questions and congratulations. Our big Canadian flag flying in the breeze let everyone know where we had started.

Near the heart of New Orleans we came to a high bridge that spanned the river. Far above us people cheered our arrival. It felt great. Our feat was appreciated.

Just past the bridge we saw more barges approaching, and one passed us at full speed not far away. We pulled up, and ended our trip, near a mass of concrete. There was no easy place to dock. We left the canoe hidden there for two days. John, a homeless young man from Atlantic Canada, slept by the Jimmy-Jock and looked after it, and I paid him for the job.

Finally we had made it, after 100 days and some 2,350 miles (3,782 kilometres) by canoe. We had been forced to drive around about 750 miles (1,207 kilometres) of river. We felt glad to be at the end, but sad too. No more would we live our carefree ways on the river, sleeping in the tent and cooking over a fire. No more would we rise with the sun. No more would coyotes or owls serenade us. The river would cease to rule our lives, and we would miss it.

As much as the river, we would miss the interesting people we befriended along the way. We had many thank-you cards to write. We were back in a mechanized world, and that meant buying a car to carry us home. While Mark explored the city I explored used-car lots, settling on a Hyundai hatchback. A motel was home for three nights.

We sampled foods, took in sights and tried to adjust to sleeping indoors. We tried to enjoy ourselves by checking out the French Quarter, taking in some jazz, eating bowls of tasty crayfish and observing the city's colourful life. The appeal of New Orleans was blunted, however, by the sad realization that our trip was over. It was the journey we enjoyed most, not the achievement of our goal.

Finally we loaded the little car and drove home. We arrived back in The Pas on Dec. 15, 1991, in time for the Christmas concert at the Neighbourhood Life Church. It was good to be home. We had lived our dream. For both of us, however, there was more paddling, and more adventure, ahead.

CHAPTER 13

THE PAS TO YORK FACTORY

In the summer of 1995, four years after Mark Bergen and I paddled from The Pas to New Orleans, I was again in a position to do a long-distance trip. Mark unfortunately was not, and neither was Larry Grenkow, my other paddling partner.

My plan was to paddle the 650 miles or 1,046 kilometres from The Pas to York Factory. The trip would take me down the Saskatchewan River to Lake Winnipeg, the Nelson River past Norway House and then the Hayes to Hudson Bay. My purpose was to retrace the route of my ancestors who had worked for the Hudson's Bay Company. Most of this region was wilderness. I agreed with Dad that from the standpoint of safety, solo wasn't the way to go. And yet I knew I could do it alone and likely have a great time. I was 36 years old and in fair shape. I had no children. (A year later I did marry.) One other potential partner came to mind: Blaine Greer.

Blaine and I had corresponded since that blustery day in 1991 when Mark and I met him in need of a tow on the Mississippi. He was working on a book about his adventures, and I wondered if he'd be interested in taking a break and trying some North Country paddling. It turned out he was, and we agreed to meet in The Pas.

Somehow our signals got crossed, and Blaine ended up arriving a few days before I did, but he made the best of it and saw some of the area. It was good to see him again. He was about 12 years older than I, stocky and strong. He still had his aluminum canoe, while I used Jimmy-Jock, my fibreglass model. Each of us was confident in his craft.

Departing from The Pas dock on June 26, we got into the current of the muddy Saskatchewan River and made good time. Soon we spotted a moose calf alone on shore, looking forlorn and vulnerable. A little later we saw a cow moose swimming, and wondered whether the two were related, and whether the cow knew where the calf was. She likely did. We also saw pelicans, a black bear and bald eagles.

Speaking of animals, each of us had one along. Blaine brought Shocker, his friendly springer spaniel, while I had my cat, Athena. Shocker seemed to enjoy the ride. He perched in the bow like a first mate scanning the seas, while Athena was more diffident. I'd have to say she would have preferred staying home. And for this trip, like our first, she kept mostly under the splash cover.

Sometimes she would surface and toss me an angry glance, as if to say, "We've been down this river before. And what's worse, you're dragging me along in the company of a blasted dog! First chance I get, I'm outta here." But she didn't bolt. She stuck by me and rode the river as best she could.

For a few days we paddled easily with the strong current. This part of the trip I know Blaine really enjoyed, as the current was similar to that of the Mississippi, and Blaine had paddled its entire length. There was chop that kept us on our toes, and there were eddies, or little whirlpools, from time to time. You don't want to let your guard down on the Saskatchewan River.

Called Kisiskatchewani Sipi or "swift flowing river" by the Cree, the Saskatchewan flows out of the Rocky Mountains across the heart of Western Canada, draining much of the region. It is formed by the joining of the North Saskatchewan and South Saskatchewan Rivers near Prince Albert. What Blaine and I were on was once a major fur-trade route, linking Great Slave Lake and the Athabasca River country to York Factory and the Red River Settlement and ultimately Montreal. It is almost 2,000 kilometres long. Several legendary figures have paddled its waters, including Henry Kelsey, who left York Factory in June 1690. With his native guides, Kelsey traveled the Hayes and Saskatchewan Rivers, wintering near The Pas before striking out overland to become possibly the first white man to see bison. (I say possibly because the Vikings could have seen them first; there was evidence of their presence in the Dakotas.) Other greats who rode the river were the La Verendrye family, Peter Pond, Peter Fiddler and Samuel Hearne.

We spotted some cabins along the way, notably at mile 18, a place otherwise known as "Wooden Tent," as I have already described. There were other cabins at miles 25, 40 and 53 (Pine Bluff fishing camp). The grassy areas near the buildings offered good tent sites and we took advantage of them. The buildings for the most part were locked.

BLAINE CONSIDERS THE NELSON

At one point it was blustery and raining, and we set up camp, each in our little zones, with our wet pets. Near the water Blaine made use of plastic and stray lumber to rig a nice shelter. The wind and rain challenged us, but we persevered. Blaine began to talk about paddling the Nelson instead of the Hayes. I was pretty firm on the latter, as that was the original plan, a prettier and safer journey than the bigger Nelson. As well, I was retracing the route of ancestors.

A drawback to the Hayes was its many portages. Blaine wasn't eager to carry his gear over them, and I didn't blame him — he hauled a fair bit more than I did, and had the dog besides. Add to the mix two independent personalities, and the result was that five days into the journey, shortly after we entered Cedar Lake, we decided to part company. This was clearly for the best. I'd wanted to slow down, fish, and render some scenes in watercolour, while Blaine preferred to get more distance done. After all, on top of all the paddling he had to drive back to Missouri. Now, each of us was free to do as he pleased.

It was funny, that first evening of the first day we paddled alone. Where did we camp? On the same shore. It was a long stony shore that faced us as we headed east, being part of a point, likely Oleson Point, that ran close to north-south. It forced us to choose between camping there and going around it — tiresome work. I arrived some time after Blaine did, as he had a fire going and his camp set up when I landed a couple of hundred metres away. We visited for a while, but kept it short as we were both pretty beat.

Cedar Lake is big water. It takes work to keep your proper track, struggle with the wind, ride the swells and make distance. I'd crossed most of the lake four years earlier with Mark Bergen, a good paddler. He and I had pulled out at Easterville and headed south into Lake Winnipegosis. This time the route would take me past Easterville to Grand Rapids, where Cedar pours into Lake Winnipeg. Cedar is a little sea, and a man is weary after a day in the sun and breeze with a paddle in his hands. By this time we'd been on the water and in the open air for about eight days, and so were eight days weary — but simultaneously growing stronger.

The landscape was stony and fairly flat. Coniferous trees predominated, but some birch, aspen and willow were about. On July 5 I rendered a watercolour of my canoe, Jimmy-Jock, on a stony shore, with an island in the background. I painted quite a few pictures, and it sure was fun. Athena enjoyed the break on land.

This whole area was under ice some 10,000 years ago, and Cedar Lake, like the others in the region, was a remnant of glacial Lake Agassiz. Similarly, the big rivers there now — Nelson, Hayes, Churchill — were once much larger as they carried melt-water to lower levels and the Arctic Ocean.

Today, people rather than nature have wrought the greatest change. The Grand Rapids Generating Station sits at the east end of Cedar Lake and interrupts the torrent of water that once spilled over the boulders toward Lake Winnipeg. It was a long carry of canoe and gear past this huge structure, and I recall some motorized help, but Lake Winnipeg finally offered up a shore. It had taken 11 days to paddle the 260 kilometres to this point.

HORSE ISLAND

Beautiful sandy beaches lined the shores north of Grand Rapids. One night Athena and I camped near a pretty creek mouth in the neighbourhood of Horse Island. While I set up the tent and got a supper fire going, Athena investigated the area's insects and various smells. She was cute as she pounced on some poor spider or something. And she was good about staying close. I helped this along by leashing her to a tree for the first while after landing each night. Last thing I wanted was an AWOL cat.

You might be interested in what a person eats on a trip like this. Living largely off the land, the staples of my diet were pike or walleye. With them I ate rice, boiled dandelion and/or common plantain leaves, saskatoons, raspberries and bunchberries, and a wild pea that grew along the north shore of Lake Winnipeg. I always kept in reserve a good store of sardines, salmon and corned beef (for the fat — the body craves fat on such a trip), some macaroni, cheese when I could get it, and bread for peanut butter and jam sandwiches. Breakfast was either cold oatmeal or any leftover mix of fish, rice and greens from the previous night. I got fresh fruit such as apples when possible and carrots as well. I thought nothing of consuming an entire cake when the opportunity arose. For anyone wishing to lose weight, canoeing is great. I looked at myself in a mirror at one point and the guy peering back was one skinny hard dude.

Plantain leaves, by the way, are a good antidote for wasp stings. The plant has a central spike and broad veiny leaves. It grows almost everywhere. Chew a leaf or two a little to release the juices and apply to the sting within seconds if you can. It works great, and I've used this remedy on two occasions.

My cookware wasn't fancy: a coffee can and a frying pan. Good quality silverware was important, though. Forget the cheap plastic stuff. Melmac plates worked well. For water, I scooped a drink out of whatever lake or river I was on — even Lake Winnipeg. I used no filter or water purification, which at the time wasn't necessary, at least for me. I remember guiding some Americans for a week of fishing along the Grass River near Snow Lake one time and suggesting they drink the water straight instead of purifying it. "That may be OK for your stomach; you're used to it," one of them said. "We're not." He had a point. A person clearly does not want the runs out there.

I killed no animals, though I carried my Ithica 12-gauge shotgun as an attitude adjuster for bears. I saw the one blackie swimming and heard one growling near a campsite, and scared him off with a shot in the air. You would have sworn it was a cannon blast, and the entire forest fell silent. The bear took the hint.

Sundays were reserved for rest. Sometimes I took a mid-week break as well. There is no sense traveling tired, as that risks injury. These rest days were good times to fish, read, explore islands, examine plant life, make bannock, swim, update the journal and reflect — activities which, though possible during travel days, were more pleasant when I was staying put.

PELICANS FASCINATE ATHENA

Up near Eagle Island, in the northwest corner of Lake Winnipeg, Athena and I saw a colony of pelicans and a congregation of various other water birds. This was a rich area for birds, proof that there was something about its food, shelter and seclusion they desired. The cat peered at the squawking masses of feathers as we passed, content to watch and hear them from afar. She adjusted well to the swells of the big lake, and I got no more angry glances as I had at the start. Maybe, truth to tell, she didn't care anymore. Can anyone really fathom the inscrutable thoughts of a cat?

All I know is, one day along the north shore of Lake Winnipeg — Monday, July 10, to be exact — she and I hit some heavy winds. I headed in as the sky darkened, and we encountered rough water as the waves built and broke along the shallow shore. This wasn't much fun for me, let alone the cat. It's one thing to ride such waves while wearing a bathing suit in an empty canoe, as my brothers Bruce and Bob and I had done in Lake Ontario at Outlet Beach Provincial Park, but quite another to do it clothed and heavy with gear. Athena was spooked, and I was none too comfortable.

We took on water as we surged toward the shore, where rocks threatened Jimmy. Waves curled over his gunnels as I steered for the softest landing. The alternative had been worse — staying out in the lake where winds and lashing rain, which appeared imminent, could cause no end of grief. Far better to land, set up camp, and prepare for a blow while you're dry. I've rarely pushed my luck while canoeing and as a result have the luxury of sitting back and sharing my journeys with you.

Yes, we were wet from wave water as we came into shore, and that didn't go over well with Athena. She scampered out of the craft and ran up the beach toward the tree line as I jumped out and hauled Jimmy Jock away from the breakers and stones. "I'll see you in a minute," I said. Famous last words.

For the next three days I searched for that cat, with no luck. What I did find the next morning at my campfire site was a pile of coyote scat — with what appeared to be hair. Coyote prints, with two claws on top, told the story. This was near the tent. I believe it was a message from the animal: "I've eaten your cat, and this is my territory, so move on." I took the 12-gauge and searched the surrounding forest and beach, calling her name all the while, for three days. Three very sad days for me.

On July 13 I wrote: "I think cat is dead, eaten. Would have come to me by now if alive. Will go tomorrow if wind permits." Tears flowed as I left that campsite the next morning. I loved that funny little cat. And now she was gone.

Disheartened, I headed on for Norway House, unwilling to lose any more time. This was wild and isolated country, and while the first 20 kilometres or so were sandy beach, the rest was mud cliffs, some of them sheer and affording no place to land. Because of this, I once paddled for 10 hours without a break. I had to stay out far enough to avoid the breaking waves. It was hard going.

On July 15 I wrote:"Wind blew till 2. Left at 4. Rain squalls developed. Few places to land. Cliff-like mud shore, some boulders. Paused at 7 to see where storm clouds going. 7:30 left and paddled to distant point, arrived 9:20...Now I can see Big Mossy Point. Two-mile channel must be close. A rugged, inhospitable shore. Steep and no place for a tent except above the cliff, where I camped tonight."

A few miles before Warren's Landing is a channel heading into Playgreen Lake. There was a cabin on each side of the channel, neither worth staying in. Playgreen Lake itself was dotted with dozens of islands and rocks near the surface — tricky even for a canoe, and I glanced off one or two.

Navigating that lake wasn't easy, and I stopped at one point on an island to get my bearings. As I stood on the rock near the water, I heard a loud squawk, then a thunk! First I looked up to see an agitated seagull. Then I looked down to see a small northern pike flopping on the granite. "This is your lucky day, Mr. Pike," I said as I slipped it back in the water. It swam away.

A few minutes later, as I explored the other end of the small island, I came across a duck blind made of tangled spruce boughs. Approaching it, I was startled when a female mallard shot out of a nest at the base of the blind, right at me. A duck nesting in a duck blind. OK.

That island had a comfortable red cabin on it, and I spent the night there. It rained. Two Cree men came up before nightfall and asked if I had any tea. I gave them some, plus some sugary drink mix for their kids, who didn't like tea. In exchange, they pointed out exactly where I was on the map. They were camped a mile away. They didn't say that I was using their cabin, but it's possible I was and they didn't want to turn me out.

TWO MINNESOTANS

In Norway House on July 19 I went to the bar for a rare beer or two. Golly they went down well. It was good to hear some music and see people again. I met two young Minnesotans who had paddled up from Minneapolis. They were retracing the route of Eric Sevareid and Walter C. Port, who in 1930 were the first men known to have done that trip.

Sevareid was only 17 at the time, Port 19. Sevareid's book, *Canoeing with the Cree*, first published in 1935, is a classic. It recounts their 14-week, 3,621-kilometre journey, which ended at York Factory just before freeze-up. It is published now by the Minnesota Historical Society Press, and remains a great read.

The two young men I met were confident — they should have been, considering how far they had come — and maybe a tad cocky. We spent part of the evening chatting in the local bar, where they were a major point of interest (especially among the women). I tipped back a couple of cool ones with them and left, as our plan was to meet at the post office at noon the next day and paddle together. For some reason they didn't show, and so I pushed off alone.

Prior to that, I saw — guess who — Blaine Greer. He told me he'd arrived some days earlier and had got a ride back to The Pas. Returning to Norway House with his truck, he'd had a mishap on one of the gravel roads and was waiting for repairs. He had seen more of wild Manitoba than most Manitobans ever do, and was ready to go home. I was pleased he'd made it to Norway House OK, as lake travel is somewhat different to the river paddling he loved so much.

UP BEFORE THE SUN

I paddled harder on this stretch because I was a bit behind schedule, having waited three days for Athena. Instead of rising at 8, I got up at 5 or 6. There were advantages to this. First, there's normally little or no wind at that hour, so paddling was easy and the miles melted away. Secondly, it was beautiful canoeing in the morning mists, watching the sun rise, enjoying the magical dawn. Third was the fact that animals often move or feed at that time, and sightings were good. It was often cold, too, at that hour, but worth it. Around 1 or 2 p.m. I often curled up under a spruce tree and slept for a while. Then, refreshed, I'd paddle till 6 or 7 p.m.

This stretch of country was remote, rugged, gorgeous. The fishing for pike and walleye was top-notch, as they hit like sledge hammers. Leaving Norway House, I headed north on the Nelson River and then branched east on the Echimamish River, which was quite narrow, only about seven metres wide in places, like the Souris, La Salle or Seine.

July 20 was notable on two counts. First, at 7:40 a.m., as the mists were rising over the river in the chilly dawn, I saw something swimming from right to left in front of my canoe. A duck? Beaver? As we neared each other it became clear that the creature was a black bear. "Hello Mr. Bear," I called out. The dog-paddling bear swam with its head out of the water and its large rear end high and dry, but everything else was submerged. At my greeting it looked at me over its left shoulder, snorted loudly and then returned its gaze forward without missing a beat. Apparently black bears swim a straight line, regardless of obstacles. Perhaps it's apocryphal, but the story is they will climb into and out of boats and canoes if necessary to maintain their course.

ౚ৵৵

The other point is that I later made a wrong turn and headed east too early, going about six kilometres up a creek, and over four beaver dams, when the water petered out. Obviously something was wrong when I had to pull the canoe through a shallow stretch in a large bog. I ended up climbing a tree to see what lay ahead, and it wasn't good. So, back I went, chuckling to myself. Hey, it happens.

After getting on the right channel I came to the first lake, Hairy Lake — an aptly named mass of bulrushes. This is also wild rice country, and I likely went through some of that. The Echimamish leads from there for about 56 kilometres until you come to a portage called Painted Stone. On the other side of this short carry the water flows north to Hudson Bay. On the west side it flows west, weakly, into the Nelson River. Hence the Cree meaning of the word: "water flowing both ways."

At the portage the rock was sheared away, blasted long ago to make the portage easier for York boats and their cargo. Apparently the Hudson's Bay Company did that some time in the 1800s when this was a major freight route. There is an old story told by aboriginal people about an alter-like rock that sat near the centre of this stone platform, at which, each year, offerings were left and figures painted.

The only people I met out there were three men in a large canoe. Hubert Folster was one of them, a fellow from Norway House. They had been fishing and he gave me a walleye, not that I really needed it, because I was catching enough on my own. But it was a kind gesture and I did not refuse it. (One thing my uncle Bert used to tell me: "If someone gives you something, accept it and say thanks. To refuse is to offend.") I took a photo of the men and it turned out well.

The next day, Sunday, July 23, I took it easy, sleeping in until noon and then painting a picture of an eagle nest at the entrance to Robinson Lake. I also caught and released a big pike and a few smaller ones, but kept two fish for supper. A west wind blew me all the way to the portage, 20 kilometres away, and my sail did a grand job. Supper was fish, couscous, bannock and honey.

Next day it was time to do the 1,800-pace (3.2-kilometre) Robinson Portage, the longest of the trip. Starting at 5:30 a.m., it took me two hours and 45 sweaty and mosquito-filled minutes to make the three carries. The old tramway used by the Hudson's Bay Company was still there, in bits and pieces. I saw an old cart that was used to carry goods on the tracks. Fireweed bloomed purple and pretty among the relics of the past.

Near Oxford Lake I encountered picturesque falls, and from one pool caught and released a 10-pound (4.5 kilogram) pike. (It was too much for me to eat.) There I met two Oxford House Crees, Norman and Ellis, and helped them haul their motorboat over the rocks. Motorboats far outnumber canoes there, now.

The area's fast water spells trouble for canoeists. In 1819, explorer John Franklin noted that "here the river rushes with irresistible force through the channels formed by two rocky islands; and we learned that last year a poor man, in hauling a boat up one of these channels, was, by the breaking of the line, precipitated into the stream and hurried down into the cascades…His body was afterward found and interred."

Near Oxford House on July 28 the wind began to blow hard. I made it down the big lake, but needed supplies, so I pulled the canoe up and left it between two boats on shore, the boats being some three metres away on either side. While up getting groceries a boy approached me. "Are you the guy with the canoe?" I nodded. "It's wrecked."

I ran down to the canoe to find that winds had apparently shifted one of the big boats over, and the two had squeezed my canoe like a vice, breaking one wooden gunnel and splitting the fiberglass almost halfway across. In other words the canoe was close to being broken in half.

On top of that I'd set my tent up nearby, expecting to sleep there because of the gale. Big mistake. Dogs tore open the screen on my door and jumped on the tent, collapsing it, leaving my waterproofing ruined and the tent wide open to mosquitoes. July 28 was not my best day.

However, because of this calamity I met a good man, Paul Dalby, manager of the Northern Store. He and his girlfriend let me stay in their home and invited me to join them for a wonderful steak dinner. Everything worked out well, as I was able to repair Jimmy-Jock the next day. For a few fleeting moments I actually considered quitting at Oxford House. In the end I had to complete the journey. By noon of July 30, in wind and rain, I left Oxford House in my continuing quest for York Factory.

ILL AT KNEE LAKE

Drinking unfiltered water too close to the community left me ill for the second time. I had the same problem at Norway House. I paddled anyway, making it up to Knee Lake, where I found a Danish family happily fishing with a guide from Knee Lake Lodge. In exchange for a watercolour painting of the lodge, owner Phil Reid, a big, blond and friendly fellow, gave me breakfast, though I still felt queasy, and was ill for four days.

At one point I saw bear tracks in the sand, and the same day locked eyes with a marten in a tree. "It's OK, little fellow," I said. He just stared.

The 10 kilometres to Swampy Lake were littered with boulders, requiring constant carrying of canoe and gear. It took me six hours to do that distance. I took great care not to turn an ankle, which would have been big trouble, and at one point did slide off a rock up to my waist in water, with no injury. I took the left passage at the north end of Knee Lake. The right passage (the passages might have simply gone around an island, I'm not sure) might have been better, I don't know. Phil Reid told me the water was down about a metre that year, so it might not have made much difference.

I took a day to rest and get ready for the most difficult part of the trip — a series of rapids and portages for 48 kilometres. It continued to rain and blow, but fortunately the wind was at my back. At Swampy Lake (which wasn't swampy at all) a family of loons serenaded me for half an hour, and I tape recorded their song — a wonderful, mystical experience. Then something moved me to stop at an island, where I found the skeletal remains of an old wooden canoe. Square nails, I noted. That would put its age at least 100 years. Dandelion grew there, a sure sign of past human presence, and I boiled some leaves with my rice and fish.

Canoeing is a metaphor for freedom. The Hayes, indeed, was liberating. See that bay? Explore it. Like that tree? Climb it. Water looks good? Swim it, fish it, drink it. The wind, your constant companion and boss, will intercede and force a day off, a day of resting and reading.

The wind carried scents of spruce and bog, mint and fire; it also carried an eagle's cry, a loon's call — and at times, I swore I heard the lingering songs of the fur brigades, boisterous and bawdy, still ringing faintly.

"Maybe the two Americans will catch up to me," I wrote. "Could use their company." Yet it was rarely lonely out there. I felt connected to the wind, the water, the trees. I rarely felt lonely, but as Aristotle said we are social beings by nature, and it would have been good to share stories and food.

I ran, lined or portaged the 48 kilometres of rapids north of Knee Lake. To line a canoe is to walk along shore and pull it using ropes attached to bow and stern. "The canoe bounced off and scraped over a lot of rocks today. I carried over one long portage, lined about six and shot about 12." Running a typical Hayes River rapid takes only about 30 exciting seconds, while portaging takes about 30 painful minutes, but can be the safer course. They were class one or two rapids, which range from ripples to rough water that can harm you. I remember running one long stretch, faring as best I could, and then at the end looking back at the white-water rock garden. It struck me as amazing that the canoe was still intact. I whispered a heartfelt thanks.

One evening, as I sat by the river eating my fish supper, I watched an eagle swoop down and pick up the carcass of a pike I'd left on a rock. An annoyed tern was on his tail, squawking.

With relief I reached the White Mud River, which marked the rapids' end. There I saw wolf tracks in the sand and enjoyed a swim in the clear and chest-deep Hayes, while admiring the towering white cliffs. Pebbles and stones lined the river bed. In 1794 a fur depot was established there, and with a metal detector I looked for relics but found none. Over the whole trip, with that detector, I found only a few large links of chain.

At this point, the Canadian Shield was behind me. I was beyond the boreal forest and into the transition zone near tundra, only three days from the Bay. Polar bear tracks told of a new animal. A storm rumbled in off the Bay, forcing me to camp for two days, marooned in the tent by wind and rain. I felt vulnerable, like a polar bear treat, soft on the outside, hard and chewy on the inside. I kept the loaded shotgun beside me in the tent.

FIVE WINNIPEGGERS

On Aug. 11, after three days of bad weather and little progress, I broke camp at 4 p.m. determined to paddle into the night. At least in the canoe

I was safer from the bears. The wind had gone down; the rain had stopped. Some hours later, as I came to the mouth of the Pennycutaway River, I saw — could it be? – yes, smoke rising from the east shore.

"Yo! You on shore! Hello!" The men stood and starred, silhouetted against their fire, stupefied to see a solitary paddler. At first, they said, they thought I was a ghost from the past.

The five Winnipeggers were Karl and Paul Gossen, Keith Eyrikson, and Chris and Dave Pancoe. They had paddled from Winnipeg to place a marker at Pancoe Lake, honouring an uncle who had died in a Japanese PoW camp 50 years earlier. I couldn't have met five more pleasant young men.

They had a duck stew simmering over the fire, and soon we were exchanging stories and eating heartily. Karl, it turned out, had a run-in with a female wolverine. He had headed out by himself to find a portage route one day, when he confronted a wolverine with a pup. Backing up, Karl found himself against a tree and could go no farther, so he snarled and became aggressive. The wolverine slowly backed away. Karl had no knife or gun. If anything, this encounter shows that wolverines are not as bloodthirsty or aggressive as folklore makes them out to be.

Another time, on Lake Winnipeg, the five were relaxing on shore when suddenly a moose came charging out of the bush and into the water beside them. Enveloping the poor beast was a cloud of mosquitoes, some of which then alighted on the five men, who joined the moose in the lake.

The six of us paddled together and arrived at York Factory at 3:30 p.m. the next day, Aug. 12. We all rejoiced; we had come a long way. My new friends had suffered the misfortune of wrecking a canoe on the rapids north of Knee Lake, and had to go back to borrow a craft from Phil Reid's lodge. One of the five, Eyrikson, paddled a kayak, and was able to outdistance us at will. (However, we would have had it over him on any portage, as kayaks are tough to carry.)

So it was with some satisfaction that we reached Hudson Bay, the first major post established by the Hudson's Bay Company about 1683. My great-great-great grandfather, James Curtis Bird, had come here in 1788 as a clerk. Finally, I had retraced some of his travels.

The five Winnipeggers and I stayed at the Blue Goose Lodge. Camping outside was not permitted, as polar bears roamed at will. In fact we had one on the deck outside our room one night. Even a trip to the outhouse required an armed escort. A few days before we got there, a bear had scooped the resident dog out of a verandah, injuring it before the young bear was shot dead by John, who ran the lodge with his wife, Andrea.

We toured the one remaining building, the Hudson's Bay Company warehouse, built in 1832, the weights and names of employees still penciled on its timbers (it was customary to be weighed upon arrival). Jim Settee gave the tour; he also stamped our paddles with the Y-F insignia, burning it into the wood. I still have that paddle, battered though it is.

We walked along the river shore, picking up old nails, spikes and the occasional piece of pottery or pipe used for smoking.

We heard about the two Americans I'd met at Norway House. Someone has seen them some distance back, stymied by the same storm. I imagine they got to York Factory OK, as I heard no news to the contrary. I'll say this, though: I was glad to be in the cabin during that cold heavy rain and not in a tent.

The weather broke, the pilot from Gillam finally flew in, and we lashed Jimmy-Jock to one of the plane's floats. From Gillam I caught a train to The Pas, where I had left my car with a friend. It was the end of a memorable and highly enjoyable summer.

But it wasn't the end of my quest to paddle the length of North America. Mark and I still had to do some 1,200 kilometres of the Minnesota and Mississippi rivers that ice and snow had forced us to miss. Two summers later, we did just that.

CHAPTER 14

BACK ON THE MISSISSIPPI

In the summer of 1997 Mark Bergen and I drove back to Le Sueur, Minnesota to paddle the 1,200 kilometres to St. Louis that we had been forced to bypass six years earlier. We were pretty excited about the trip because it meant closure to us, the completion of an important task.

Mark was now a student at the University of Saskatchewan's College of Veterinary Medicine in Saskatoon. As he observed, "We both knew that one day we would finish the stretch we had missed between Le Sueur, Minnesota and St. Louis; it was just a matter of when. The summer of 1997 turned out to be perfect timing for both of us. The winter of 1996/1997 found me well on my way toward my goal of becoming a Doctor of Veterinary Medicine. One night the phone rang and one of my roommates yelled that it was for me. It was Brad. As soon as I heard his voice I knew why he was calling and what my answer would be."

As we drove into Le Sueur that hot July day, we didn't know where we would leave the car. But we needed groceries, so we pulled into the parking lot of a local store, my red canoe riding proudly on top.

"Nice canoe," said a smiling middle-aged man, as we walked to the store.

"Thanks," I said.

"You paddling the river?" he asked.

"We are. In fact this is our second time here. The first was during the Halloween Blizzard of 1991."

"Are you the two Canadians who got stuck in that storm?"

"We are," I said. "You remember that?"

"For sure. By the way, my name's John — John Chamberlain."

John was a retired banker who owned land just outside of town. He offered to let us park my Volvo station wagon at his place for the six weeks we would be away. It worked out great. John and his wife were good to us. John contacted his friends at the *Le Sueur News-Herald*, the paper that had featured us on their front page in its coverage Nov. 6, 1991 of the Halloween Blizzard. A new editor, Daryl Thul, came out and interviewed us. "Blizzard boys return" the headline announced. The story read in part:

"If the picture above this story looks strangely familiar, it's probably because you've seen if before. Excepting the fact that last time the pair on the side of the canoe — Brad Bird and Mark Bergen — were standing up to their knees in snow."

Next day our hosts drove us to a little park beside the river, where we began our trip.

LITTLE PRESSURE

The trip went smoothly, partly because the weather was awesome — day after day of warm sunny weather — and partly because Mark and I were six years older. We were more at ease with each other, and with ourselves. Both of us were more settled. And there wasn't the pressure to go hard and fast to beat the weather that dogged us earlier. We had six weeks, plenty of time to get the job done in a leisurely manner, about 29 kilometres a day. Easy.

As I glance at a map to refresh my memory, the names of familiar places appear: Shakopee, Red Wing, Lake Pepin, and Lake City (where I shaved, and we went into town and used the Internet thanks to a shopkeeper to send a photo back to a friend, Dave Wall). There were Wabasha, La Crosse, Dubuque, Bellevue and Clinton. Davenport, Muscatine, and Fort Madison (where we were not allowed to tie up to a city dock, in one of the few times we encountered inhospitable rules). Keokuk (an Aboriginal name of a great warrior), Quincy and Hannibal.

Hannibal is promoted as the home of Mark Twain, and we enjoyed a tour of the town and its sights. I'll never forget the conversation we had with the gent who ran the harbour. When he asked where we were from, we told him Winnipeg. He wasn't clear on Winnipeg. "That's not far from Minot, North Dakota," I said. Oh, he knew Minot. A former boss of his had been promoted and transferred to Minot to run an operation there. He asked this gentleman, a colleague at the time, to join him. "I'll do a lot for a friend," he told us, "but I will not move to Minot! It's too darn cold up there." We laughed.

USED-BOOK STORES

Great memories. Simple camps. Freedom. Stews over the fire. Wonderful swims.

Mark and I rose in the morning knowing our only real task was to paddle some miles and enjoy life along the way. We stopped at old riverside towns such as Guttenburg, Davenport and Red Wing. Most were friendly to boaters, with small docks and stores close by.

We'd head into town, each with a task to get either water or food. Then we explored used-book stores, general stores, museums and libraries for about an hour. I picked up some good books, including *Journal of a Trapper* by Osbourne Russell, who worked the foothills during the 1830s. Another was The *Old North Trail*, the life, legends and religion of the Blackfeet people. This was by Walter McClintock, who was with the Blackfeet on their reservation. He became the adopted son of a chief and learned about their past.

We were delighted by the cleanliness and clarity of the Upper Mississippi. I tasted the water with no ill effect. Somebody told us the city of Minneapolis had recently invested $1 billion in its sewage treatment system, and it showed. People thronged to the river on weekends and even during the week (on their holidays, no doubt), boating and camping on the sandbars.

That's another thing Mark and I enjoyed — the sandbars. It made easy work of tramping around our camps in bare feet, and the sand was white and fine like that of the Bahamas. It did tend to get into our food and tent, but what are a few pits when life is a bowl of cherries?

Mark recalls how the river was a local playground. "We discovered that the Mississippi is a major source of recreation for many people during the summer, particularly near the city of St. Louis. The closer we got to that city, the more the river swarmed with activity — houseboats, motor boats, fishing boats, jet skis, paddlewheelers and floating casinos. On some sandy islands there would be countless houseboats anchored or tethered, with children playing in the water and innumerable jet skis roaring around. I remember one hot sunny day while we were swimming, a big paddlewheeler tour boat roared past us, heading downstream. On a whim I yelled over to Brad, 'Hey, I wonder if we could pass that boat if we tried!' We clambered back into Jimmy Jock (this involved careful balancing, one of us on each side to prevent capsizing) and began to paddle with all our might. We began to gain steadily, and presently the tourists began to notice the silent race. Before long a sizeable crowd was cheering us on from the top deck of the paddlewheeler (and I hate to admit this, but we were clad only in our briefs). One old boy hollered out 'Where you fellas from?' and the answer generated even more interest from the onlookers. We paddled with machine-like precision until we were satisfied that we had soundly defeated the paddlewheeler."

Yes, that was a great race. The boaters too were friendly, sometimes asking if we needed anything. Once a boat with two men came by.

"You guys wanna get stoned?"

"No thanks," I said, "we're not into that, but we could sure use a cold beer!" — and we got a beer.

Another time when docked, I must have looked pretty hot and bedraggled because a man stopped on the dock and peered as I sat in the stern. Mark was getting supplies. "You look like you need a beer," he said. I hadn't shaved in three days, my straw hat was torn and askew, my jeans were filthy and, like Mark, I was literally fried. He plucked one from his cooler and handed it over. In exchange I answered his questions about the trip, and he said he envied us.

The swimming in the Upper Mississippi was superb. Rather than stop at a sandbar, we jumped out of the canoe in mid-channel and continued to make distance while cooling off. The glorious water literally sucked the heat from our bones. We usually swam three or four times a day, as a reward for distance. Mark often swam after supper as well, where we camped.

During our mid-channel swims the current continued to carry us south, and we'd sometimes drift quite a ways while playing like a couple of otters. It was liberating to be free of the canoe. Getting back into the moving craft involved "humping" our bellies over an end, and then swinging a leg up into Jimmy.

THE CHAIN OF ROCKS

Our entry into St. Louis was memorable. And we wouldn't have had it any other way. A few days earlier, a boater had stopped to chat and warn us about a barrier at St. Louis called the Chain of Rocks. This was a natural barrier that created a rapids. The man warned us not to try it, but to take the circumventing channel instead. However, at the final lock and dam before St. Louis we asked about it and were told we could safely run it. We were also told that the channel lock was backed up, requiring a long wait. And so we opted for the Chain of Rocks — against the previous good advice — figuring the high water (two metres higher than normal) would keep us off the boulders.

We sailed down the river, clipping along at about seven m.p.h. after the Missouri River poured into the Mississippi and added to its considerable flow. We saw the big plain sign that read, "All boats enter here." In our hubris we did not enter. We guffawed that this didn't apply to Jimmy-Jock.

A large bridge spanned the river just before the rapids. As we approached it, I knew there was no turning back. The current was too strong. We were being swept along. I heard a honk or two from the traffic so far overhead, and unbeknownst to us at the time, somebody was phoning the authorities.

First we saw a bit of turbulence. Then it looked pretty rough, as the water foamed and frothed. I stood up and scanned the river for the best available chute and found one to our right. "Ride it like you do your horse, Mark," I said. Mark was quite a cowboy. We knew that we didn't stand much of a chance of floating out the other end — at least in an upright canoe!

We hit that chute and then the curling waves below it, exiting not badly, but then we hit another rapid with frothing waves that poured into Jimmy, filling us in a flash. Then I was bobbing in the water, one hand on Jimmy and the other on our tub that carried our valuables. I looked around for Mark and saw him surface. "Mark, are you OK?"

"Yes!" he said. "What a rush! Let's do it again!" We hadn't hit any rocks, and all of our gear was floating except for my favourite sandals, which had sunk. Even the clothes we'd been drying on our Action Packers were fine, as the plastic boxes floated among us, the current all the while taking us toward an island.

As we laughed and talked about emptying the canoe, a boat arrived with two fishermen, and they started to retrieve our floating gear. We were thankful, but also a bit annoyed. We had things in hand, and we preferred to get ourselves out of our own pickles. The men were naturally concerned and told us the Chain of Rocks had taken lives. Were we OK? Yes, we assured them. I actually had to ask them to relax; we were fine, and having a grand old time, too. They deposited us on that island after collecting our flotsam, and we began to dry gear.

A little while later a big official boat approached and called to us from a megaphone: "Have you seen the canoeists who went over the Chain of Rocks?"

"Yeah!" I replied. "We're them! And we're fine, thanks!"

"OK. No problem. Just keep paying your taxes!" We didn't have the heart to tell them we were Canadians.

BAREFOOT IN ST. LOUIS

Next morning, on Aug. 18, we landed in downtown St. Louis, 1,207 kilometres from our starting point after six weeks on the river. The Arch — huge and impressive, signifying the gateway to the West — stood nearby. Lacking shoes, I went barefoot in St. Louis. Despite this I got into the Arch, and wandered around the museum barefoot, prompting the occasional glance of disapproval. Then we tried a fancy restaurant, as we had talked about our celebratory meal. The security guy was firm. No shoes? No go. There was no place close at hand to buy any.

Finally we found a bar and grill and had a fantastic lunch. It was a scene right out of Cheers. Some professional dudes in suits plied us with questions and we had some good laughs retelling our recent adventures. The good thing was, the counter we sat at was close to the door, and I don't think anyone was aware of my feet until we left.

BACK IN LE SUEUR

We picked up a rental car and drove for 12 hours, arriving in Le Sueur in heavy rain. We slept in the car for three hours, and then drove to the farm where my Volvo was parked. John Chamberlain welcomed us heartily and gave us breakfast, after which we drove to Minneapolis, dropped off the rental, and then drove home to Lake Metigoshe on Turtle Mountain.

What a great trip. We gave Jimmy-Jock a personality, calling him Jimmy "The Terminator" Jock, imagining that his photo was in the cabin of every barge captain on the river. They trembled at the mere mention of the dreaded Mean Mark, Bad Brad and Jimmy-Jock, who cleaved barges like a knife through butter. Upon hearing we were near, the captains responded as follows. First they peed their pants ("How do you suppose the river got so high?" Jimmy asked). Then they passed wind. It was true there was always a breeze wherever we were. It was also true that the barges avoided us. One time a barge captain honked at us and came close, and I said, "Jimmy never backs down from a challenge!" Mark laughed. That may have been what started our fantasy. It was hilarious in the circumstances, as we were so flimsy compared to those giant steel barges.

With all three portions together, it was a journey of some 6,000 kilometres, from the Arctic Ocean to the Gulf of Mexico. That is far from being the longest canoe trip on record. For years the Starkells' 12,000-mile (19,300-kilometre) odyssey held that distinction. It was never our purpose to try for any record. Our purpose was to seek adventure for its own sake. And I think you will agree we found what we sought. People need excitement, which is why carnival rides and special-effects movies are popular. Let's face it, the predictability and static nature of normal day-to-day life can be boring. Personally, I need the authentic excitement of a long journey — meeting new people, seeing new places, escaping close calls, chasing a goal — to feel I'm truly alive.

If the trip wasn't that long, it was distinctly North American, and it has not been duplicated, to my knowledge. The northern portion, with its isolation and rapids, will discourage many. And so it should. Life is too precious to be foolishly risked. Good skills and good sense are needed up there. In my view, the southern part of the Mississippi was also a high-risk exercise, given the fog, whirlpools and man-made hazards along the way. Whatever else it was, the journey was a happy time in my life. I'm so glad I did it.

Mark sums up our shared portion of the trip. "I remembered the first day, Sept. 1, 1991, leaving with a crowd of onlookers wishing us well. The short jaunt along the Saskatchewan River before it flowed into Cedar Lake. The traversing of Lake Winnipegosis and Lake Manitoba with Athena the cat peering out from under the tarp, and the incident when she was attacked by the old farmer's dog. The short stay in Winnipeg with my aunt and uncle. The gruelling three weeks paddling up the winding Red River against the current. Crossing the continental divide and starting on the Minnesota River. Surviving one of the worst snowstorms in Minnesota's history, having the river freeze up and then risking our lives in an ice jam at Lock and Dam 13. Being forced to skip a significant stretch of the Mississippi because of ice conditions. Inching steadily south and experiencing the gradual changes in climate and culture. Memphis. Arriving in New Orleans, with people waving overhead from a huge bridge. And all the people we met along the way, from Cree fishermen in northern Manitoba to little old grandmothers in North Dakota to tugboat captains in Louisiana. As the famous Arch of St. Louis came into view, it brought closure to one of the best experiences of my life."

Amen to that.

APPENDIX

Canoe camping is one of the great pleasures of my life, and it is enjoyed by many thousands around the globe. But like anything else there are things you can do — and things you can know — to enhance the pleasure of your trips. Here are some tips and values I embrace.

First, quality matters. But that doesn't mean you have to go out and buy all the newest equipment and technology. In other words, just because it's new and high-tech doesn't mean it's best for you. An example is canoes. Yes, Kevlar is good because it's light, durable and strong. But a good used fiberglass canoe that costs you 10 or 20 per cent of what you'd spend on a Kevlar craft can be just as good or better — and you'll feel great by having saved some cash. Personally, I prefer fiberglass to Kevlar because I know I can repair it. Yes, on a longer trip you need to carry a repair kit and the necessary tools and know how to use them. This is a small price to pay for self-sufficiency 200 kilometres from the nearest help.

I have never bought a new canoe. In fact, I have purchased only one canoe in my life, the Jimmy-Jock, as you have read about, for which I paid $200 in 1986. Two other canoes I salvaged from a dump and repaired. The first canoe I used as a boy was bought by my parents. In my adulthood, I have never felt the need for a canoe other than Jimmy-Jock. Some people collect canoes the way others collect sweaters and shirts, and that's OK as long as you can afford them and properly store and maintain all those craft. Maybe they would be better off given or sold to others who could enjoy them.

Quality also matters with respect to your duffel bags and clothes, but again, these do not have to be high-tech. What I am saying is that canoeing is a great activity because even those of us on limited incomes can take part by purchasing shrewdly and by making use of many things we already possess. For example, the pack I use on trips was my father's Second World War duffel bag issued by the Air Force. You might find a similarly useful bag at the local Goodwill Store or church bazaar or at a garage sale. But I did go out and buy special waterproof sacks (one fits inside the duffel) in which to store sleeping bags, clothes and the tent. These three sacks have been invaluable. For clothes, I like wool in cool weather. Toques and mitts are good to have along for sleeping comfort, even in summer. Polyester slacks dry much faster than blue jeans and are much lighter. Nylon pants are excellent. For rain gear, I purchased an expensive Gore-tex jacket (which is breathable, meaning it releases body moisture) that has served me well for two decades. Many times during storms I was glad to have it.

The key to getting a bargain is knowledge. Know ahead of time what you need or want. List such items — maybe you need a new life-jacket and hat, as I do — so that when you see them at a garage sale or whatever, you grab them. I once saw a pair of cross-country ski boots at a sale held by the Manitoba Naturalists Society and knew immediately they were for me, because I'd catalogued what things I needed. I've used those boots for years. It's no good thinking after the fact, "Gee, I could have used that paddle. It would have made a nice spare and they only wanted $5 for it." So consider what things you could use, think about them, dream about items you would like to have but would never buy new, and you'll be ready when the opportunity presents itself to acquire them affordably (maybe for free).

Tents. Get a good one. Any old tent will do when the sun is shining and the temperature is fine. The real test of a tent is what it does when things turn bad. So buy quality, take care of it, and learn how to use it well. I still have my old Woods canvas tent that I bought in the mid-1970s. I like canvas. However, I also have a newer nylon tent that also does a good job. Regardless of the material, pack it dry and clean and take care of it. Air it out later if you have to pack it wet.

Be careful where you put the tent. Avoid low spots. Even the best of tents cannot keep all the water out in a low spot. Use well-drained areas that will catch the morning sun and offer protection from prevailing winds. Beware of old trees. They can fall down in winds or drop large branches. Also beware of what you put your tent on. Grass is best. I don't put my tent on sand if I can help it. It takes forever to get rid of the stuff, and it gets into your food. Beware of thorns. Mark Bergen and I were in a cow pasture in North Dakota when we unwittingly put our tent on some briars. They punctured its polypropylene base and that led to some uncomfortably wet times, as you can imagine. Eventually I had the bottom entirely replaced. So beware not only of what is above your tent, but also of what is below. This includes sharp sticks, and even garbage. Once, when inspecting the ground, I found an old knife. Garbage is everywhere.

Waterproof your tent as needed every year or two. Do not tighten ropes excessively, as this stresses seams. Loosen a canvas tent in a rain, as canvas tightens. Dry tents thoroughly whenever possible and make sure the tent bag is also dry. Water will lead to mildew, which means trouble.

Partners. Most of the time we can choose our partners. Choose well. You are stuck with these people, their values and their habits, for the duration of your trip. That can turn a good trip into a nightmare. Sometimes, though, such as in group situations, we lack control over who goes with us. Be charitable, cheerful and forgiving. This is God's way of teaching patience. At the same time, if the group is clearly about to do something you know in your gut is wrong for you — such as run a rapid instead of portaging around it — then stick to your guns and do what you think is right. Your life could depend on it. One time in Winnipeg I was with a group that was taking a short trip along one of the city's minor rivers in the spring. The river was fast and full. I had misgivings about the journey, but didn't express them, not wanting to rock the boat, as I was not one of the leaders. Two canoes capsized by colliding with sweepers — trees that extend out from shore. We got the people safely on land, but it was a close call. In hindsight, I should have spoken up.

Don't fight the weather. The wind is your guide and your master, not some opponent to be defeated. I generally don't travel in bad weather. It's just not worth the risk. Looked at in another way, the energy you expend to travel 10 kilometres on a bad day would get you 30 kilometres on a good one. So rest, read and sleep in your comfortable tent on bad days. You'll make up the distance on the good days when the wind is light or at your back.

Cooking. In bear country it is best not to sleep where you eat supper (for what should be obvious reasons). Eat at one location, which usually means a fire, and then paddle on to a new site. This separates you from much of your supper smell, but not all, as it will cling to your clothes. I got into the habit of "washing" my clothes regularly (by plunging them in and rinsing them, usually from the canoe) in whatever lake or river I was on when in bear country. When traveling alone through the wilderness of northern Manitoba where black bears were present, I generally cooked my supper at about 7 p.m. (typically a fresh fish), and then paddled on for an hour or more to a tent site. With this method, I was never visited by a bear.

Speaking of bears, in wilderness tripping I made a habit of sleeping with my shotgun and sheath knife handy. I mean to say, right beside me. Predator black bears do make up a small but important percentage of the species. With any luck, you will never encounter one. There is a big downside to carrying firearms, and that is the risk of an accident. In all my years of paddling I have never shot a bear. Only once did I fire the weapon to scare one off. Essentially I didn't need to carry a gun — but might have.

Don't depend on fish for food unless you know you can consistently produce. Carry an adequate supply of dry foods or canned foods to sustain yourself. Remember that your appetite will expand from all the exercise and fresh air. I always carried sufficient food on solo trips, and Mark and I always had something good in reserve on our way to New Orleans. When we went up and over the bank to farm houses in North Dakota, it was to buy food to prevent us from having to use our last resources.

Take care of your gear. Paddles should be leaned against a tree or placed gently in the canoe, not tossed down on the rocks. The problem with this is that gouges from such mistreatment could give you slivers and/or blisters. Also, a wooden paddle could crack, and then break when you really need it. We always carried a spare and we used traditional wooden paddles. Some people like the bent paddles. Please yourself.

Respect people and the environment. Do not throw fish guts into the water. They take a long time to decompose in water. Leave them on a rock or shore some distance from a campsite for the gulls and minks and skunks and crows to clean up within hours. I've seen even bald eagles snatch fish guts when they can. Once I came upon a lovely wilderness campsite and decided to have a swim — only to find dozens of disgusting perch carcasses littering the water. I found out who had done it (a teacher and his class) and wrote a letter to the editor, I was so mad. I also leave my tent sites clean. As well as being an eyesore, garbage is a threat to others because it pulls in bears, skunks and the like that learn to make the site a regular part of their rounds. One day they might return and find YOU camped there. So burn it or pack it out.

We all hate to lose things. Try identifying items prone to being lost with orange tape. I wrapped a piece around my saw, put a piece on one end of my Action Packer to indicate which end had the peanut butter, tied tape to tent ropes I tended to trip over, etc. It's useful stuff.

Keep it simple. Keep your expectations modest for daily travel. Keep your route simple if you are just starting out. Talk to local paddlers about good canoe routes in your area. Owners/managers of sporting goods stores are also good sources of information. Keep your fishing tackle simple, too. I carry only a few Mepps hooks and a spoon or two and some extra leaders when on a long trip. Because my line and reel are in good repair and my drag is set properly, the chances of losing a lure (and hence a fish) are minimized.

That's another point: while you hope for the best, plan and prepare for the worst. Mark and I had it so that everything either floated or was waterproof or both. I like to use two Action Packers, which fit so well in most canoes. One carries our food; the other carries cooking utensils, repair kit, some food and other gear. The tent rides between them on the bottom of the canoe at the centre thwart. Because it is in a waterproof bag, it is fine there. The duffel carries my clothes and sits behind the stern seat, serving as a backrest when needed. Mark's plastic barrel, which carried his clothes, rode behind him up front.

Which brings us to the loading of a canoe. You should be a little stern heavy, bow light, for best control and speed. I stress "a little." Test your load until you have it all placed for the best effect. A common problem among neophytes is to bring too much stuff. Remember, if your trip involves portages you have to carry that sleeping cot time and time again. And all that booze. Are you really up to it? One of the great things about canoe camping is how it simplifies our lives, shedding us of unnecessary clutter. Keep that in mind when packing.

Keep your load low. Anything above the gunnels will catch the wind and slow you down, or even stop you cold. Remember the fellow Mark and I towed on the Mississippi River? The wind caught his gear sail-like and literally blew him to shore. Our canoe was sleek in comparison and as a result easier to paddle into a wind. A low load is also safer because you have less chance of tipping with a lower centre of gravity.

Finally, don't forget the toilet paper. I like to have two rolls, one in the food box and another in my clothes bag. Both are kept in plastic bags and sealed. Leaves just don't cut this mustard.

I remember reading somewhere about why we tend to feel so much at ease in the wilderness. It's because that is the world God created, untainted by humans. There could be something there. We need wilderness for our souls. Let us preserve it always.

THE LEGEND OF JIMMY-JOCK

There's a story on the river that is told at fireside,
That will send a chilly shiver through the toughest captain's hide,
It is not a myth 'bout whirlpool or legendary rock,
But the saga of a vessel called the mighty Jimmy-Jock.

Through the ages, down the decades, many's been the boats of lore,
That have worked the mighty Mississip, a well-respected chore,
But the barges and the tugboats that have pushed the water high,
Take a backseat to the Jimmy-Jock, a very special guy.

I say "guy" because he talked and felt and hurt like one of us,
'Cause he had a personality, unusual it was,
For a boat to be a person just like me and just like you,
Jimmy is a special case, you see, no regular canoe.

His grandpa was a river barge, his grandma was one too,
But his daddy was a York boat large, his mother, a canoe.
A cedar strip canoe and in her day she was a prize,
When his daddy took a look at her he couldn't believe his eyes.

A product of this union, Jim was strong and bold and tough,
He could go where things were easy, he could go where things were rough,
He would laugh at churning rapids, he would enter them with glee,
For he knew that when he rode them he felt absolutely free.

First he sailed the mighty Nelson, then the Hayes, Saskatchewan,
Working for a trapper known as Billy Absalon.
How he loved those early years when he and Billy searched the North,
For the furs of beaver, otter, wolf, all of substantial worth.

They would travel near the tamarack, the spruces and bunchberry,
They would feast upon the saskatoon, its juices sweet and cheery,
They would drink the cool clean waters of the many rivers north,
As they chased the furs that were, back then, all of substantial worth.

One time as Billy Absalon turned Jimmy down a creek,
It became a raging river, flowing fast and cold and sleek,
Then some boulders, big and ominous, appeared within their view,
And it looked like Bill and Jimmy soon would say adieu.

There was no way round those boulders, there was no way they could stop,
They would have to run the rapid, where the chilly waters drop,
They would have to risk the rocks that surely held in store, my friend,
Broken bodies, broken hearts, and a very sorry end.

Jimmy faced the coming struggle with a calmness in his heart,
For he knew that for all living things the time comes to depart,
But he wished, oh how he prayed, that he could somehow learn to fly,
Somehow lift old Billy and his gear up to the clear blue sky.

He rode the river, praying hard for magic wings of flight,
Then a bull moose at the water's edge did see a funny sight,
For the red canoe that held a man, his gear and fur so high,
Left the water, cleared the rocks — that canoe began to fly!

"I am flying!" Jimmy shouted as they cleared the nearby spruce,
"You are flying!" Billy blurted as they passed a puzzled goose,
On they soared, above the Jack pines, to the sun and back they went,
On a magic trip that left them happy, weary, spent.

From that time whenever rocks intruded in their water path,
Jimmy flew them far above them, far above their watery bath.
Like a fire in an old growth did his fame and story spread,
Till the time when Bill the trapper, old and gray, was found quite dead.

My father was a fisherman who worked Lake Winnipeg,
When one day he took a break for lunch, or just to rest his leg,
He pulled up to Billy's cabin near a creek and spooked a fawn,
Where he found the stiff old body of the trapper, Absalon.

There was nothing he could do to change the fact that Bill was dead.
But he wondered 'bout the fate of the canoe, he dubbed Old Red,
So he took it home for me, who then was 10, a little lad,
And he swore that when he did, the old canoe, it looked less sad.

When I saw the magic vessel known to me as Jimmy-Jock,
I could hardly trust my very eyes, it was a pleasant shock.
"Dad, that canoe is famous and already has a name,"
And I went on to explain its most extraordinary fame.

It wasn't long thereafter that I took a little trip,
To the river known by many as the Mighty Mississip.
With Jimmy-Jock beneath me and my paddle dripping wet,
We set off for some adventure just to see what we could get.

With the river on his belly and the sunshine on his back,
My old Jimmy was a happy lad on his new watery track,
For it seemed his grandpa's spirit as a river-going barge,
Still lived on in little Jimmy, whose own heart was extra large.

When he saw a barge approaching he would boldly stare and shout,
"Let us move that bully over, that big bully, that big lout,
He takes up most all the river, pushes us right to the shore,
We'll show him a thing or two, a thing or two and more!"

THE LEGEND OF JIMMY-JOCK

That's when Jimmy charged the barge despite my efforts to desist,
Putting up a fiery effort that no human could resist,
He was set upon his fateful task to terminate that boat,
Sending crew and coal and colours all across the river afloat.

If I hadn't seen if for myself, I wouldn't have believed (would you?)
That a 16-foot canoe could cleave a monstrous barge in two,
But cleave he did, that barge did split —
And fall into the Mississip.

It took another time or two when barges split like seasoned wood,
'Fore captains learned to stay away from Jimmy-Jock for their own good,
They named him well, wrote on a rock,
"Steer clear of Jim, 'The Barge Terminator' Jock."

Many's the tale of barges and gales the Mississippi has seen,
But few will equal this chilling sequel to Jimmy's flight over green,
He flew to save his trapper friend when rocks did threaten their run,
Then learned to cleave big bossy barges, giving him much fun.

His legend made, he retired to Turtle Mountain, Manitoba, Canada,
Where he rests in shade.
You can still hear him laugh, though, and see him grin with glee
As he remembers his Mississippi days, and the barge captains he made flee.

— By Brad Bird, Sept. 4, 1997.

(Mark Bergen and I, as we paddled down the Mississippi in 1997,
imagined Jimmy-Jock as a "Barge Terminator" and had fun doing it,
as you can imagine. I penned this poem upon our return.)